THE
VEGAN
8

THE VEGAN

8

100 *Simple, Delicious*
Recipes Made With
8 *Ingredients or Less*

.....

≫ **BRANDI DOMING** ≪
Creator of **The Vegan 8**

Oxmoor
House®

❧ CONTENTS ❧

©2018 Brandi Doming

Photos on pages 34, 127, 136, 159, 193, 194, 201, 202, 205, 206, 210: ©2018 by Brandi Doming

Design and remaining photography: ©2018 by Time Inc. Books, a division of Meredith Corporation

Published by Oxmoor House, an imprint of Time Inc. Books

Senior Editor: Rachel Quinlivan West, R.D.
Project Editor: Lacie Pinyan
Editorial Assistant: Lauren Moriarty
Design Director: Melissa Clark
Photo Director: Paden Reich
Designers: Alison Chi, Teresa Cole, Alana Hogg, Matt Ryan
Photographers: Antonis Achilleos, Caitlin Bensel, Jennifer Causey, Greg DuPree, Alison Miksch, Jason Wallis
Prop Stylists: Kay E. Clarke, Audrey Davis, Heather Chadduck Hillegas, Christine Keely, Mindi Shapiro Levine, Claire Spollen, Kathleen Varner
Food Stylists: Margaret Monroe Dickey, Emily Nabors Hall, Anna Hampton, Ana Kelly, Karen Schroeder-Rankin, Tina Bell Stamos, Chelsea Zimmer
Senior Production Manager: Greg A. Amason
Associate Manager for Project Management and Production: Anna Riego Muñiz
Copy Editors: Rebecca Brennan, Dolores Hydock
Proofreader: Jacqueline Giovanelli
Indexer: Mary Ann Laurens
Fellows: Holly Ravazzolo, Hanna Yokeley

ISBN-13: 978-0-8487-5707-6

Library of Congress Control Number: 2018941158

First Edition 2018

Printed in the United States of America

10 9 8 7 6 5 4 3 2

For information on bulk purchases, please contact IPG at specialmarkets@ipgbook.com or call (800) 888-4741.

DEDICATION

I dedicate this book to you, my readers. It is because of you who make my recipes every single day and have remained loyal for so long, that this book is possible. Thank you to those who have put their faith in me and my ability to create recipes that you and your family, vegan or not, have loved. Thank you for your endless support. I am so grateful to each and every one of you.

WELCOME

When I look back on my life, it's so surprising that I've written a vegan cookbook. If you had told me a few years ago that I would become vegan, I would have laughed. I grew up in Texas where we lived off of animal-based meals in my family. There was meat and dairy at every meal.

My journey to becoming vegan was unexpected. My husband suffered for years from debilitating gout. It was through many painful years, sleepless nights, conflicting advice from doctors, and being on and off crutches that I discovered our own answer and truth in how to heal him. I started to research a vegetarian diet and, ultimately, a vegan diet. To our amazement, after going fully vegan by October of 2012, his gout began to go away. Our lives changed dramatically in a wonderful way. Who knew a lifetime love for cooking and baking was the perfect preparation for our new path? I had been writing recipes for years, so transitioning to plant-based recipes was an exciting and natural next step for me.

This new life gave me the idea to start a blog. At the beginning of our journey, I had started a vegetarian blog, but shortly after becoming vegan I craved a new direction. In October of 2013, *The Vegan 8* was born. After looking through my previous vegetarian blog, I discovered that my most popular recipes were 8 ingredients or less. A light bulb went off! Could I successfully run a blog using so few ingredients in not only desserts but also savory recipes and beyond? It was scary, for sure, but I truly believed that I could reach more people and show them how easy and delicious vegan food is. To my amazement, it grew more than I ever imagined, and here we are.

We all have busy lives, especially families with children, and when it's time for a meal it doesn't need to be complicated. I love proving that you don't need a ton of time or a long list of ingredients to eat healthy, homemade meals that will satisfy you and not overwhelm you in the kitchen. Each of the recipes in this book and on my blog is made with just 8 ingredients or less, not including the very basics of salt, black pepper, or water since we all have those in our pantry. The ironic part is when you think of simple food, you might think boring. Nope! I focus on classic dishes and comfort foods made easy that satisfy vegans and non-vegans alike. Honestly, it's just good food. I hope you come to love this book and the recipes as much as my family has.

—Brandi Doming

THE VEGAN 8 KITCHEN

I love bold flavors but also enjoy simplicity. In this chapter, you'll find the ingredients that I keep stocked and use regularly in my kitchen to create satisfying recipes with just 8 ingredients or less (not including salt, pepper, or water). I may use the same or similar ingredients in my recipes, but I like to use them in new and exciting ways each time. You will find a full yet pretty recognizable list of spices, which is intentional; I'm not going to send you off looking for days for a spice you probably have never heard of. If you are new to vegan cooking or even cooking in general, this list of ingredients is a good starting point to stock your pantry. From there, you'll be able to make a wide range of quick and easy meals from this book.

GETTING STARTED

FOLLOWING THE RECIPES AND SUBSTITUTIONS

Let's start with the most important thing: Read the entire recipe before beginning each one so you are prepared and know what to expect. This will make following the recipe more comfortable, and you'll avoid surprises during cooking. Additionally, since all of my recipes use 8 ingredients or less (not including salt, black pepper, or water), then you can imagine how important each ingredient is for the end result. I chose every ingredient very carefully for maximum impact and spent hours in the kitchen perfecting the recipes so that you don't have to. You can simply follow the recipe to create a meal that I hope you will love! So, if you try to sub 4 of the 8 ingredients, you are going to end up with a completely different recipe—and you may not like the results. Plus, if you alter the recipe on the first go, then you won't know what the intended result is. The finished dish could be bland or the dessert may not bake up properly. I'm all for adapting things to suit your tastes (I have notes about this very thing throughout the book), but here's my advice: I strongly encourage you to follow these recipes exactly as written at least the first time you make them. After you get a feel for the flavors and method, feel free to add your own twists thereafter.

As for substitutions, I do list subs in recipes throughout the book when they can be done to make a recipe gluten free and nut free, for example. But, in many cases, that sub is never going to taste as amazing as the original recipe, which includes the ingredients I think make the finished dish taste the best and have the best texture.

For example, with cashew-based recipes, white beans or potatoes are listed as subs for those with allergies,

but (in my opinion) those subs don't taste as rich or creamy as cashews. Of course, I have many readers who are used to using white beans in place of cashews and enjoy them, which makes me happy! Also, another common nut-free sub I give for my desserts is to use sunflower seed butter in place of almond butter. The texture will be basically the same, but sunflower seed butter does leave a much stronger flavor, which I note on those recipes.

If you ever have any questions or concerns, I'm always here to help. Please don't ever hesitate to reach out to me through my website's contact page, and I will answer any questions you have. You can find me at TheVegan8.com.

WEIGHING INGREDIENTS AND USING A SCALE

I am a staunch advocate of weighing ingredients. The reason is simple: accuracy. Have you ever heard somebody say that the first time they baked something it was great, but the next time it didn't work? I hear that all the time. While there are many factors, it is likely because everyone measures ingredients a little differently. The results can be all over the place. Use a scale, and your chances for mess-ups will go down considerably. That's why I include weights in every recipe—it ensures my recipes work perfectly each time you make them. The only time weighing ingredients is not necessary is with small teaspoon amounts, which are often so small that the scale does not detect them accurately. So, for anything below a tablespoon, I still rely on my measuring spoons. Also, a kitchen scale is a small kitchen investment, starting at $10 and up. Mine was only about $20, and I have used the same one for years.

BAKING

BAKING LOVE

I'm a lifelong baker, and I have been writing decadent dessert recipes long before I ever became vegan. Creating desserts has always been a passion—I blame my obsessive sweet tooth for that. I let my creativity explode with desserts. I first started falling in love with baking from cookbooks. I would play around with those recipes, change things up, and try to make them a bit healthier. Even years back, I was swapping out part of the oil or butter for zucchini and fruit purees like applesauce.

BAKING AND WEIGHING

Have you ever heard, "Baking is a science"? Well, it's true. Some science experiments are cool and some are explosions. That is why some people *hate* baking and others love it. But that's also why using a scale becomes even more important. I nearly want to shout it from the rooftops, "Use a scale when baking!" Why? We all measure flours a little differently. Some people pack the measuring cups, while others do not. But that difference can be the reason for the results you get, be they breathtaking or simply awful. Even 1 or 2 tablespoons of flour or liquid can tremendously affect the end result and texture of a baked good. Accuracy in measurements (as well as quality recipes) will yield happy bakers.

The thing is, once you get into the habit of weighing your ingredients, it is so much faster and easier. I just plop my bowl onto the scale, add the flour, salt, baking powder, and then the liquids and the rest of the ingredients. I never even touch a measuring cup. Just be sure to zero out in between each ingredient, and you are good to go. When weighing ingredients with liquids, make sure to pour slowly so you don't add too much too fast and throw off the liquid ratio. It may seem a bit weird at first if you've never weighed ingredients, but it will soon become second nature. Plus, you will come to love the tasty results that follow from your precision. So, to recap, go out and buy a scale before making the recipes from this book, OK?

DIFFERENT PANS FOR BAKING

The pans you use play a crucial role in the results since heat reacts differently in each one. The pan called for in each recipe is the one that yields the best results.

Aluminum vs. stone or ceramic: Aluminum pans are great conductors of heat—they heat up and distribute heat very quickly and effectively. However, the pans are thin and, depending on the recipe, that can mean the edges sometimes crisp quicker than desired. For example, for Crowd-Pleasing Brownies on page 211, I use a ceramic or stone baking dish. Why? I use cornstarch in the recipe, which helps give nice crispy edges that are classic in brownies. But cornstarch also causes baked goods to brown quickly, which is why an aluminum or nonstick dark metal pan is not best. Those pans will heat up the edges quicker and cause them to burn before the center is cooked through. With a stone dish, the pan and the brownie batter heat up slower, resulting in evenly cooked brownies. But the opposite is the case with Showstopper Chocolate Cake on page 192. That recipe doesn't use starch (only flour), and it is quite a thick cake. In this case, an aluminum pan is what we want. It heats the cake quickly and evenly, and it cooks perfectly throughout. A stone dish can cause the centers to take longer to cook through.

Muffin pans: With muffins, I use both a nonstick and a ceramic muffin pan. I love both and don't find the differences to be too significant. Plus, I almost always use liners. If you coat a dark pan with nonstick spray and don't use liners, the outsides of the muffins will crisp quicker, which actually can taste pretty yummy. I don't use silicone pans because the flavor and texture is compromised.

Sheet pans (nonstick): When baking cookies, dark metal pans brown the bottoms best. Dark metal pans heat up quicker and hotter, giving cookie bottoms a blast of heat for a better crisp and texture. Aluminum sheet pans work, too, and I use mine often, so it's OK if that's all you have. Use them knowing that they may take another minute to bake or the bottoms might not get quite as crisp.

MY PANTRY

SPICES & HERBS

Allspice: This spice is used in a lot of chai recipes and Jamaican food. It has a very strong, warm taste and gives great depth of flavor to food with just minimal amounts added. I use it in my Spice-Is-Nice Baked Oatmeal Squares on page 43.

Dried basil, oregano, rosemary, and thyme: I use these quite often in my cooking and in several recipes in this book for Italian-flavored dishes. I tend to make my own Italian seasoning blend with these herbs and keep it on hand for quick meals. Everybody should have these on hand.

Cardamom: This is another spice that tops my list. It is fairly strong and comes from the seed pods of several different plants of the ginger family. This is why it is often paired with other spices like cinnamon, ginger, and nutmeg—think chai (like in my Chai-Spiced Almond Caramel on page 220 and Chai Spice Blend on page 236). Cardamom can be used in both savory and sweet applications, but it can be overpowering if too much is used. One of my favorite uses is cardamom paired with orange.

Chili powder: Meet one of my favorite spices. American chili powders are typically a blend of paprika, onion powder, garlic powder, oregano, and ground chiles

or cayenne pepper. Brands can vary, but they are similar enough in flavor to use interchangeably. It is what is commonly used in the United States when a recipe calls for chili powder. In other countries, chili powder is very different. It refers to an ingredient that is much hotter and is usually just all chiles or peppers. For my recipes, it's important to use the American-style version that includes a combination of spices but no added salt. If you cannot find a standard American-style chili powder where you live, then make my easy homemade version on page 245.

Chipotle chile pepper: This is made from dried and ground peppers. As you can imagine, it is quite spicy. It adds lovely dimension and a bold zest to recipes, but a little goes a long way. Be sure to start out with less and add more at the end as needed. I especially love the flavor this spice adds in My Favorite Barbecue Sauce on page 99.

Cinnamon: My favorite flavor when it comes to desserts is cinnamon. I'm a spice lover, and while I have some close seconds, this one tops them all. Cinnamon is warming, slightly sweet, and can work beautifully in both sweet and savory recipes, especially curries. One of my favorite recipes in this book that uses cinnamon is the Spice-Is-Nice Baked Oatmeal Squares on page 43.

Cloves: This is a very strong spice. A little goes a *long* way. However, it is a distinct flavor that is so amazing and simply cannot be replaced. In fact, try my Gingerbread Latte on page 223 and see just how amazing and rich this spice is. It wouldn't have the same flavor without the small amount of cloves.

Coriander: This is the dried and ground seed of the cilantro plant, but it tastes nothing at all like fresh cilantro leaves. So, if you hate cilantro, fear not. This has an awesome flavor—an almost sweet taste—that is great in curries, chilis, and soups. Be sure to check it out in my Green Split Pea Soup with Coriander on page 150.

Cumin: This spice lends a warm, smoky note to recipes and is commonly used in Mexican dishes. I love to use it in chilis, soups, and, of course, Mexican-inspired dishes or where I want a similar flavor.

Curry spice blend: I love the rich, bold flavors of curries so much that I created my own Curry Spice Blend on page 242, which is used in the Protein-Packed Curry Chickpeas and Sweet Potato Rounds on page 118.

Garlic powder: This is speedier than mincing garlic. It definitely is a different flavor than fresh, but it is great when you need something quick and in sauces and dressings where you don't want bits of garlic.

Ground ginger: I ove this spice. I profess my love to it every time I take it out of my cupboard. OK, maybe not, but it is so delicious and gives such depth of flavor to both savory and sweet dishes. I especially love it in my Gingerbread Latte on page 223.

Italian seasoning: I love this blend of dried herbs and use it often. Most stores sell it, but be sure to pick up a blend without added red pepper or salt, as it will drastically affect the flavor of my recipes. If you cannot find it, then use the DIY blend I list in the *Tip* below each recipe that calls for Italian seasoning.

Nutmeg: This spice is great for pumpkin breads, gingerbread, and holiday baked goods. I use it in my Pumpkin Pie Spice Blend on page 238.

Onion powder: This is made from dried onion that has been ground. It doesn't taste at all like fresh onions, but it is a good staple to have in your pantry for added flavor in dishes. I love the taste of it in my All-Purpose Lemon Cream on page 100.

Regular paprika: Similar to smoked paprika without the smoky part, this paprika is mild but adds a lovely deep flavor and warmth to dishes.

Smoked paprika: I have a deep fondness for this spice. I adore smoky flavors (thanks to a childhood spent eating a lot of smoked sausage and chili, which will be rather evident in this book), and this stuff is just magical. It is

simply made from peppers that have been dried and smoked. Can you say "yum"? It lends itself well to hearty or "meaty" types of recipes. I especially love it in my Secret Ingredient Three-Bean Chili on page 165.

Red pepper flakes: If you don't like heat, then you are probably not a fan of this one. They are also called chili flakes. Again, use sparingly to start with since it can overpower a dish and really burn your mouth.

❧ tip ❧

It's best to use spices that are fresh and not more than a year old for the best flavor. It's a good idea to do a quick check of your spice cabinet every few months to see what needs to be tossed and restocked.

◀◀◀◀

LIQUID FLAVOR ENHANCERS

I'm all about making things easy, but sometimes I prefer to create my own homemade versions for some commonly used liquids, such as salsa, barbecue sauce, or teriyaki sauce. They taste fresher, while also being healthier. While you can always use your favorite store-bought brand to keep the recipe strictly at 8 ingredients, there are certain recipes where I recommend my homemade versions for best results. Plus, my homemade versions usually take about 10 minutes to make!

Barbecue sauce: My favorite flavor for savory dishes is barbecue sauce. You will notice the depth of my love for it in this book. For any and all of my recipes featuring barbecue sauce, I use two sauces. Both are featured in this book: Emergency Smoky Barbecue Sauce on page 226 and My Favorite Barbecue Sauce on page 99. The recipes that use either will be noted accordingly.

Liquid smoke: Liquid smoke gives an incredible smoky flavor to recipes like Emergency Smoky Barbecue Sauce on page 226, Smoky White Bean and Potato Stew on page 162, or chili. There really is no replacement for this. It can be found at most grocery stores.

Dijon and regular yellow mustard: I use these mustards to add depth of flavor to sauces and soups. The Dijon does some wonderful flavor magic in the Cajun Veggie and Potato Chowder on page 158.

Red curry paste: This is used in Thai red curries and adds exceptional color, flavor, and heat. Make sure to use a vegan one—I love the Thai Kitchen brand.

Salsa: I use and love salsa like it's my J.O.B. There are a few recipes that call for your favorite salsa in this book, but I'd like to direct you to my Restaurant-Style Chipotle Salsa on page 104. I think it's the best homemade salsa ever. It's like the kind served in a good Mexican restaurant. Go make it right now.

Soy sauce: I always use low-sodium soy sauce in my recipes. I find it is still plenty salty and has incredible flavor. If you are gluten free, then make sure to use a wheat free variety like tamari. One of my favorite recipes using soy sauce is my Thai Rice Noodle and Bok Choy Soup on page 154.

Teriyaki sauce: Teriyaki sauce is amazing on veggies, rice, or as the main flavor component of a burger! I make my own—Sesame Teriyaki Sauce on page 229—but feel free to use a store brand to make the most amazing burgers ever using my Teriyaki Patties recipe on page 137.

Tomato sauce/puree: This is made from pureed tomatoes, and I use it in soups and to make homemade spaghetti or pizza sauce. It offers lots of flavor and a beautiful color. I buy brands that are just tomatoes and salt, no other added ingredients. If possible, buy the kind sold in glass jars or boxed cartons, as they don't leave a metallic taste like the cans do.

Vanilla extract: It is always a good idea to have a huge bottle of this stuff in your pantry for any time a baking craving hits.

Low-sodium vegetable broth: I use this for soups and to cook veggies in. It is good to always have some in your pantry. I always buy the low-sodium varieties so I can control how much salt goes in my food.

Apple cider vinegar: This vinegar is used in many recipes like dressings or sauces (see my 20-Minute Alfredo on page 68) for an added depth of flavor. It is a great ingredient to keep stocked.

Dark balsamic vinegar: I choose this vinegar when white or apple cider vinegar won't work as well in the flavor department. It is simply amazing in my BBQ Chipotle Green Lentils with Potato Wedges on page 117.

White vinegar: I use this vinegar to make things taste like cheese. It works remarkably better than apple cider vinegar. See my Silky Smooth Chive and Dill Cream Cheese on page 47 and Pizza Quesadillas on page 83.

Vegan Worcestershire sauce: You can find vegan Worcestershire sauce at Whole Foods, Sprouts, or Amazon. I have used the following brands: Wan Ja Shan, Annie's, and The Wizard's—all work well. Please note that the Wan Ja Shan brand is the only one that is gluten free and vegan; the other two are not gluten free.

SWEETENERS

Agave nectar: This comes from the agave plant. There is a lot of controversy about the dangers of agave and, honestly, I don't think too much about that. To me, any sweetener is bad if you use too much. I rarely use it, except when I don't want a strong maple flavor. Agave syrup is also much less expensive than maple syrup, so for those who want a more budget-friendly option, agave is the next best sub. It is a bit sweeter and more neutral in flavor, which is why it's not my go-to liquid sweetener. I simply prefer the depth of flavor that maple syrup offers. You can find it at pretty much any grocery store these days or online. It will say "agave nectar" or "agave in the raw." Just make sure you don't buy a version labeled "light," as it tends to have additives and not a very good flavor.

Maple syrup: This is my #1 go-to sweetener (I use it for most of my desserts). I rarely ever use white sugar for my recipes as I prefer less refined sweeteners. Make sure to use a pure maple syrup—none of that imitation nonsense—which is unrefined, natural, and tastes amazing. Maple syrup can be pricey, but it's worth it for the flavor payoff.

Unsulphured molasses: This is a very thick, sticky sweetener that isn't very sweet at all but rather on the bitter side. It is a great addition to spiced baked goods or in barbecue sauce. It provides a wonderful, rich flavor and, when paired with a sweetener, it tastes amazing.

Coconut sugar: This is my second most used sweetener. Regardless of its name and origins (it comes from the sap of the coconut tree), it doesn't taste like coconut at all. It has a caramel-like flavor, kind of like brown sugar but not nearly as sweet. It is very gritty, though. It's not as fine as granulated sugar nor as sweet, so you'll need a bit more in recipes to get the same sweetness. One of my favorite recipes is the Toffee-Pecan Glazed Cake on page 195 that uses this sugar as the main flavor.

Raw sugar: I usually reserve this for use as a pretty coating for cookies. I use the large brown granules labeled "in the raw," which give a lovely sheen and crunch to baked goods. See the Bakery-Style Blueberry Muffins on page 39 and My Favorite Gingersnaps on page 207.

NON-DAIRY MILKS AND YOGURT

Cashew milk: This milk is made with raw cashews and water. I like to make my own (see page 246) because the store-bought varieties simply cannot compare to the taste, texture, and consistency achieved in homemade, and it only takes about a minute to make in a high-powered blender. Homemade can't be used in all recipes because it is so thick, but those recipes requiring homemade will be noted, like the Cajun Veggie and Potato Chowder on page 158. If I happen to use store-bought versions for a recipe, it is in a baked good.

Full-fat coconut milk: The only recipes that make me reach for full-fat coconut milk are curries—my favorite is Easy One-Pan Red Curry with Spinach and Carrots on page 71. Full-fat coconut milk yields a creamier sauce, and the coconut flavor goes well with the spices traditionally used in those dishes.

"Lite" coconut milk (low-fat): This is one of my go-to milks because it is creamy but not excessively so, like the full-fat version. It is the milk that's most similar in texture to dairy milk, but the coconut flavor is so mild that it is not detected in the finished dishes. Also, since I do not use oils in my recipes, "lite" coconut milk provides moisture and richness that almond, rice, or oat milks simply can't achieve. My favorite brand is Thai Kitchen, which is widely available. It is always creamy, smooth, and not watery like so many brands. "Lite" coconut milk has around 3 to 4g of fat per serving, while full-fat clocks in around 11 to 14g.

Soy milk: This milk is made with soybeans and water. Thanks to its creamy texture and fairly neutral flavor, I use it a lot—you'll see it listed often throughout this book. I recommend the WESTSOY brand since it has no additives.

Non-dairy yogurt: I use both soy and coconut yogurts throughout this book because they provide incredible moisture and texture to sauces and baked goods. I love the Silk soy yogurt brand and the So Delicious coconut yogurt brand.

NUT BUTTERS (FATS)

I do not use oil in my recipes. The only exceptions I make in this book are for cooking pancakes and sometimes for spraying a pan. I prefer to get my fats from whole-food sources like nuts, seeds, milks, avocados, and olives, among others. This way, I'm getting the benefits the entire food offers, including protein, carbs, fiber, and myriad vitamins, minerals, and health-promoting compounds. Oils provide 100% pure liquid fat and nearly twice the calories and fat as nut butters. So, all the recipes that are listed "oil free" in this book mean that no oil is *added* to the recipes. This does not refer to the oils found naturally in foods such as seeds, nuts, or chocolate chips.

Almond butter: You will notice I have quite an addiction to almond butter. I use it in place of oil or butters in my recipes—it provides the richness of oil but offers a better depth of flavor. For my recipes, use a super-creamy, almost drippy almond butter for best results. If I'm not making my own (see my recipe on page 234), I buy the Simple Truth brand from Kroger, which is exceptionally creamy and runny and has no added oils, sugar, or salt. If you do not have Kroger in your area, Sprouts carries the MaraNatha brand. But if you can't find either, just make sure to use a really smooth variety that has no added oil, sugar, or salt—the runnier, the better, as the overly thick, stiff

kinds don't blend very well. The oils tend to settle at the top, so when opening up the jar, just mix it up really well before using in the recipes. If you use a lot of almond butter, you may want to transfer it to a larger jar to make stirring much easier. That's what I do!

Cashew butter: I love, *love* cashew butter. It is made strictly from raw cashews and is what I like to use in sauces and homemade cream cheese. It is not a nut butter that can be replaced with others. It has a much lower oil content than almond butter and also firms up really well in the fridge, so there isn't really a sub for it that will work nearly as well. I like to make my own since it is nearly impossible to find raw versions without added oil or sugar. It's so easy! You just need a food processor. See page 247 for the recipe.

Peanut butter: I don't use peanut butter often, but sometimes it is a flavor that I want in a recipe that no other nut butter can provide. An example of this is my Thai Peanut-Sesame Sauce on page 88. In a lot of recipes, it can be subbed with almond butter or sunflower seed butter if there is an allergy.

Sunflower seed butter: This is made from raw or roasted sunflower kernels. It has a similar taste and texture to peanut butter and is listed as a nut-free sub for many recipes in this book that call for almond butter. It is not as naturally

sweet and can be a bit bitter though, so I recommend using a sunflower seed butter that has added sugar and salt but no added oil for best results. I love the SunButter brand—it is the only one I use. Because of its assertive flavor, please note that using sunflower seed butter will leave a sunflower seed butter taste in my recipes.

NUTS AND SEEDS

The nuts and seeds I always keep stocked in my pantry (and that are used throughout this book) are raw cashews, sliced almonds, pecans, pumpkin seeds, sesame seeds, chia seeds, ground flaxseeds, poppy seeds, and sunflower kernels.

NUT FREE

The recipes that don't include tree nuts will be clearly listed as nut free. As a note: This does not include coconut since it is technically a drupe, or fruit, and not a nut. Since many people who cannot eat nuts can eat coconut with no problem, I have not omitted it from recipes identified as nut free in this book. For many recipes, I've also provided a nut-free sub. Those include sunflower seed butter, seeds, white beans, and potatoes. Please keep in mind, though, that those subs are only recommended for those with an allergy since the subs will never have the same amazing result as the original recipe.

FLOURS

Blanched almond flour (gluten free): This gluten-free flour is made from skinless almonds that have been blanched in boiling water. It produces a light and fluffy texture in baked goods and, thanks to its high fat content, lends moisture. Since I don't use oils in my recipes, almond flour is a wonderful replacement, providing richness and a very slight nutty taste. It is very important to use a superfine blanched almond flour in my recipes. The difference is very noticeable, as some brands are rather gritty, which leaves a gritty taste and a denser, flatter result—not the light and fluffy baked good we're all craving. For cookies, a grittier flour will make the cookies less smooth.
It is crucial to use a good brand, especially with cakes. My brands of choice are Honeyville, King Arthur, or—if you live in Texas—the HEB brand. As much as I love Bob's Red Mill products, I've not had good results with the almond flour. Despite being labeled "superfine," I've found it to be rather gritty, and it doesn't produce the light, fluffy results I want.

Cornmeal: I use fine cornmeal in this book for both my Sweet Potato Cornbread on page 179 and My Favorite Savory Meatless Bean Balls on page 133. It yields a wonderful texture and has incredible binding qualities.

Oat flour and oats: This is made from ground oats and is gluten free when certified gluten-free oats are used. Make sure to buy brands certified as gluten free if needed. (I use Bob's Red Mill.) I use this flour often at home and in some of the recipes in this book. It's a healthy, nutrient-dense flour that gives a wonderful texture to baked goods. Because it can also make baked goods really dense, I always combine it with another flour or starch for the best texture. Make sure to have quick-cooking oats on hand for a few of the recipes in this book, as they help give the bean balls in the Ultimate BBQ Bean Ball Sub on page 138 a lovely meaty, chewy texture. Regular old-fashioned oats are too large, and I've found that when grinding them up myself it's easy to overdo it, making it too much like a flour.

Whole-wheat pastry flour: Not to be confused with regular whole-wheat flour that's milled from hard wheat, this flour is milled from soft wheat. The two are very different in texture and cannot be subbed for one another. Neither is gluten free. The protein content is lower in pastry flour, producing the softest, most tender, beautiful cakes. In fact, the two recipes in this book that count on this flour are both cakes: the Toffee-Pecan Glazed Cake on page 195 and the Showstopper Chocolate Cake on page 192. The chocolate cake is so fantastic that this recipe alone makes it worth the cost to buy the flour. If you are not gluten free, then please go buy this flour. It can also be found online and in the flour aisle of many grocery stores.

Brown rice flour (gluten free): This gluten-free flour is made from milled brown rice. I use Bob's Red Mill. This flour has a more distinct flavor, so is best in recipes where it is masked well by the flavors of other ingredients or used in smaller quantities. It is my go-to flour for thickening sauces, and it leaves no odd taste behind. I do use it in baking, like in my Chocolate Lovers Double-Fudge Cookies on page 204 and my Bakery-Style Blueberry Muffins on page 39. However, it can cause things to be rather crumbly or dry, so it's best used with other binding ingredients, other flours, and enough fat to combat its dryness.

White rice flour (gluten free): This gluten-free flour is made from milled white rice. I use Bob's Red Mill or the HEB brand. It is fantastic for gluten-free baking. It binds exceptionally well—much better than brown rice flour—and it doesn't have an off-taste like brown rice flour. Not to mention, the color is bright white just like regular all-purpose flour, so it won't alter the color of your baked good.

It works really well in cookie recipes both for binding and creating a lovely chewy texture. When used in cake recipes, it does best when combined with other flours and starches, as it usually causes the final product to be gummy and/or gritty if used as the sole flour. You will find it in my Crowd-Pleasing Brownies on page 211 and Magical Chocolate Chip Cookie Bars on page 208.

Spelt flour: While this flour contains less gluten, it is not gluten free. Unlike those with celiac disease, many people who have gluten sensitivities can tolerate spelt because of the lower gluten content. If you have celiac or extreme gluten intolerances, it is not suitable for you. I love spelt flour because, when paired with other flours or starches, it produces light and tender results. However, when used alone, spelt flour produces baked goods that lack structure and crumble more easily, thanks to its low gluten content. It also does not rise as well as regular wheat flour or all-purpose flour. It has a fairly strong flavor, so it should be paired with other ingredients that help mask the flavor. My favorite recipes that use spelt are the Bed-and-Breakfast Pumpkin Pie Crepes on page 32, the Baked Pumpkin Spice–Chocolate Chip Donuts on page 200, and the Double-Chocolate Fluffy Pancakes on page 35.

STARCHES

Cornstarch: This very light and fluffy powder has exceptional binding qualities in baking, adds lightness, and also helps to give crispy, browning effects. But beware: Too much will cause your baked goods to be excessively chewy, so a good amount of fat is needed to counteract that. I like to use this starch because it is inexpensive and easy to find. If you live outside the United States, cornstarch is labeled as corn flour.

Potato starch: Potato starch and potato flour are entirely different, so make sure you read the label closely when buying it. The starch is extracted from potatoes, whereas potato flour is made from whole potatoes that have been dried and ground. I never, ever use potato flour. It is very heavy and will add a

truckload of moisture to the dish as well as making it taste like potatoes! The starch, however, makes gluten-free baked goods very tender and light. I love, *love* to use this starch in baking, and I find it has magical powers when it comes to pancakes. See the Double-Chocolate Fluffy Pancakes on page 35. You can, however, sub with cornstarch in most recipes

and it almost always works very well since the two are very similar.

Tapioca starch: This starch is extracted from the cassava plant. It has great binding and thickening qualities. In baking, it helps to replace eggs, as well as give a crispy, browning effect. Too much, though, and you'll end up gnawing and chewing on a tough and gooey cake or muffin.

OTHER INGREDIENTS

This list doesn't include every single ingredient in this book, but it shares what ingredients (aside from the spices and nuts already mentioned) are often used in my kitchen—the ones I keep stocked for easy, quick meals.

Unsweetened applesauce

Avocados

Baking powder

Baking soda

Beans and legumes: This includes black beans, chickpeas, white cannellini beans, pinto beans, red beans, red lentils, and green lentils.

Bell peppers

Broccoli

Carrots

Chocolate chips: I stock dairy-free and semisweet. I love both the Enjoy Life and Guittard brands. Just make sure milk is not an added ingredient.

Cocoa powder

Frozen sweet corn

Garlic cloves

Fresh ginger

Fresh herbs: basil, cilantro, or your favorites

Jalapeños: fresh and sliced from a jar

Lemons and limes

Sliced black olives

Green onions: I use these quite often as a garnish.

Onions: both red and yellow

Pasta: all kinds

Poblano peppers

Potatoes: Yukon Gold, russet, and sweet potatoes

Canned pumpkin (unsweetened)

Brown long-grain rice

White jasmine rice

Spinach

Tomato paste

Tomato sauce

Low-sodium vegetable broth

MY KITCHEN EQUIPMENT

I'm not going to name off everything I have in my kitchen, but these are the main items. Not every single one of them is needed for this book, but most are. If you follow my blog or do so after buying this book, it is good to have all of these. You probably have most of them already.

8-inch square baking pans: Buy both aluminum and stone.

High-powered blender: I use a Vitamix.

Cake pans: For cake baking, it's best to have both 8- and 9-inch round pans.

Cast-iron skillet

Chef's knife

Large cutting board

Food processor: I love my 11-cup Cuisinart.

9- x 5-inch loaf pans: Buy versions in nonstick, ceramic, and stone.

12-cup muffin pan

Sheet pans

Stainless steel pots and pans (medium and large)

Storage containers and jars: I keep all of my nuts and flours stored in these, both for ease of use and a longer shelf life.

Vegetable peeler

Whisks: Get them in both small and large sizes. I prefer wire over plastic or silicone.

✌ 2 ✌

BREAKFAST

I must admit that I don't always follow that golden rule of "never skipping breakfast." In fact, it has become a normal thing. Before I know it, it is lunchtime each day and I have reached the *hangry* stage.

This is surprising, as years ago breakfast used to be my favorite meal, and I never, *ever* would skip it. But, as a busy blogger and a mom, things change. However, when the weekend rolls around, I always cook pancakes or waffles for my family—that is a tradition we don't skip. When I do make breakfast, I like hearty and impressive ones. So, for this chapter, I wanted to share breakfast recipes that are extremely delicious and are sure to impress family as well as guests.

BED-AND-BREAKFAST PUMPKIN PIE CREPES

PREP: 10 minutes
COOK: 18 minutes
YIELDS: 6 crepes

. . . .

1 cup (128g) spelt flour
1½ teaspoons (4g) pumpkin pie
    spice or Pumpkin Pie Spice
    Blend (page 238)
1 teaspoon (5g) baking powder
⅛ teaspoon fine salt
1 cup (240g) soy milk or other
    plant-based milk
¼ cup (80g) pure maple syrup
¼ cup (60g) pumpkin puree

OPTIONAL: fresh fruit,
    powdered sugar, cinnamon,
    coconut whipped cream
    for serving

tip

If you cannot find pumpkin pie
spice, make my easy
DIY blend on page 238.

Plain crepes are yummy, but sometimes I like something a bit more exciting. Crepes that have the flavors of pumpkin pie? Yes! This recipe, made with pumpkin pie spice, maple syrup, and cooked pumpkin, gives a nice twist to traditional crepes and reminds me of a special breakfast you would get at a bed-and-breakfast.

1. Add the spelt flour, pumpkin pie spice, baking powder, and salt to a large bowl, and whisk very well until thoroughly mixed.

2. Add the milk, syrup, and pumpkin, and whisk until smooth. The batter should be runny. Please note that all milks have different flavors and will affect the flavor and consistency somewhat.

3. While your batter sits for about 5 minutes, heat a 10-inch nonstick pan or a crepe pan over medium-low heat. It must be a nonstick pan.

4. Once the pan is hot, spray with nonstick spray. Pour about ⅓ cup of the batter onto the pan, and immediately and quickly, pick up the pan and swirl it around so the batter forms a large, round, thin shape. If the batter is not spread out thin, your crepes will be too thick and will break easily. Cook the first side for 2 to 3 minutes until the bottom is golden brown, and then carefully flip the crepe over using a large spatula and cook another minute or so on the second side.

5. Repeat with the remaining batter. If you are new at making crepes, sometimes it can take a couple of trials to get down the method, but don't worry, practice will get you there.

6. To serve, fold the crepes in triangles or roll up. For a true bed-and-breakfast presentation, I love to add some fresh fruit, dollop with whipped cream, and sprinkle with freshly grated cinnamon and powdered sugar, and then place everything on a tray. Serve with coffee and juice and it's pure heaven.

. . . .

Nutrition per crepe: 141 calories | 1.4g fat | 4.1g protein | 27g carbs | 3.3g fiber | 9.4g sugar | 132mg sodium

. . . .

DOUBLE-CHOCOLATE FLUFFY PANCAKES

These aren't your ordinary boring pancakes. These are the ones you whip out to impress guests and especially kiddos—they make you feel like you are eating chocolate cake for breakfast! They are a bit sweeter than regular pancakes, as they are meant to be, which counteracts the bitterness from all of the cocoa powder in them. I like to use my griddle for this recipe so I can cook all the pancakes at the same time. When working with flours, I always recommend a scale for accuracy since we all measure differently.

1. Add the spelt flour, cocoa powder, potato starch, baking powder, and salt to a large bowl, and whisk well. Pour in the milk, syrup, vanilla, and chocolate chips, and stir with a spoon gently until combined. Don't overmix. The batter should be fairly thick and smooth but not stiff. If you measured by weight, the batter should be just right, but if it seems stiff, add another tablespoon of milk. You don't want a thin batter though or that will make thin, dense pancakes.

2. While your batter sits for 10 minutes, heat a griddle or nonstick skillet over medium-low heat, closer to low. It's important to let your batter sit, as it allows the starch and baking powder to react with the liquids and yield fluffy pancakes.

3. After the 10 minutes and once the pan is hot, stir the batter just once more. Spray the griddle or pan with nonstick spray. Pour about ¼ cup of batter per pancake onto the hot pan but do not spread it out (this helps them cook up fluffy).

4. Cook for 3 to 4 minutes or until the edges are looking dry and the top is forming bubbles. Flip the pancakes, and cook another 1 to 2 minutes on the other side or until golden. If your pancakes are browning too quickly on the first side, slightly lower the heat. Repeat with the remaining batter, if needed. Serve with fresh strawberries and maple syrup.

. . . .

Nutrition per pancake: 183 calories | 4.1g fat | 3.6g protein | 35g carbs | 4.2g fiber | 13.3g sugar | 275mg sodium

. . . .

NOTE To make this gluten free, sub both the spelt and potato starch with 1 cup + 3 tablespoons (190g) King Arthur Flour gluten-free (and gum-free) all-purpose flour. Don't use a blend with added gums, which will ruin the texture. This blend is rice- and starch-based. I've only tested this blend and cannot vouch for other subs. If you cannot find potato starch, then sub with cornstarch. No other starches are recommended. Also, since there is no oil or much fat in this pancake batter, "lite" canned coconut milk is necessary because it has the right amount of fat to yield the best fluffy and moist texture. Do not use the carton kind; it is full of gums and vitamins and will ruin the texture. Full-fat coconut milk will make the pancakes too dense, while other milks will yield a chewy texture.

PREP: 10 minutes
COOK: 10 minutes
YIELDS: 7 large pancakes

. . . .

1 cup (128g) spelt flour
¼ cup (24g) natural unsweetened cocoa powder, sifted
3 tablespoons (30g) potato starch
2 teaspoons (10g) baking powder
½ teaspoon (3g) fine salt
¾ cup (180g) canned "lite" coconut milk, shaken first
6 tablespoons (120g) pure maple syrup
1 teaspoon (5g) vanilla extract
3 tablespoons (42g) mini semi-sweet dairy-free chocolate chips

OPTIONAL: fresh strawberries, maple syrup for serving

ORANGE-VANILLA WAFFLES

PREP: 10 minutes
COOK: 18 minutes
YIELDS: 6 (7-inch) waffles

. . . .

1¾ cups (224g) gluten-free fine
  oat flour
4 tablespoons (32g) cornstarch
1 tablespoon (15g) baking powder
½ teaspoon (3g) fine salt
¾ cup (180g) freshly squeezed
  orange juice
1 cup (240g) canned "lite"
  coconut milk, shaken first, or
  cashew milk
4 tablespoons (80g) pure maple
  syrup
1 tablespoon (15g) vanilla extract
6 tablespoons (96g) creamy
  sunflower seed butter (such as
  SunButter) or roasted almond
  butter

I'm a huge pancake lover, but waffles are equally delicious to me. Nothing can beat a crispy waffle on Sunday morning. My all-time favorite recipe is my chai waffles from my blog, so I used that recipe as a base to create this variation with the light and refreshing flavor combo of fresh orange juice and vanilla. I love these finished with a drizzle of maple syrup and served alongside some fresh orange juice, coffee, and fruit. If there are any leftovers, I like to crisp them up in my toaster oven the next day.

1. Add the oat flour, cornstarch, baking powder, and salt to a large bowl, and whisk very well until thoroughly incorporated.

2. In a separate medium bowl, add the orange juice, milk, syrup, vanilla, and sunflower seed butter, and whisk until smooth. Pour the liquids over the dry, and whisk just until mixed and smooth. Don't overmix. Let the batter sit while you heat up your waffle maker. (I used a 7-inch round waffle maker. Batter amounts and yield will vary based on the size of your waffle maker.) The batter will thicken some as it sits.

3. Spray the top and bottom of the waffle maker with nonstick spray. (They will stick if you don't.) Pour about ⅔ cup of batter and quickly spread out the top with a spoon, being careful not to spread it too close to the edge to prevent overflowing. Cook for 3 to 5 minutes or until the waffles are crisp. Repeat with the remaining batter. Waffles are best eaten immediately as they do soften if they are left out awhile.

. . . .

Nutrition per waffle: 349 calories | 14.2g fat | 10g protein | 46.9g carbs | 5.3g fiber | 13.1g sugar | 433mg sodium

. . . .

➤ tip ➤

You can sub spelt flour or regular all-purpose flour for the oat flour. Spelt has a strong taste, which is why I prefer oat flour. Regular all-purpose is more absorbent, so you may need to add a little extra milk if the batter is too thick. As far as the nut butter, you can use almond butter if you don't have a nut allergy.

BAKERY-STYLE BLUEBERRY MUFFINS

What qualities do muffins need to be considered bakery quality? To me, they should be tall, fluffy, tender, light, perfectly sweet, and have a gorgeous golden sugar topping. These muffins have all of the above. The yogurt and cashew milk give the same richness to these muffins that you would find at a bakery. If your taste buds are so inclined, chocolate chips make a great sub for the blueberries. It's important that your liquids are at room temperature so your batter is smooth and the muffins are tender and light.

1. Preheat the oven to 375°F (190°C). Spray 10 muffin cups with nonstick spray or use nonstick liners. (Using just the sprayed muffin tin without liners will yield the more classic muffin top.)

2. Add the oat flour, rice flour, baking powder, and salt to a large bowl, and whisk well.

3. Add the syrup, milk, and yogurt, and stir very gently just until combined. Be careful about overmixing the batter, which can result in dense muffins. Gently fold in the blueberries. The batter will be fairly thick but smooth.

4. Divide the batter evenly among the 10 prepared muffin cups. The batter will be filled high. Sprinkle each top with about a teaspoon of the raw sugar.

5. Bake at 375°F for 20 to 25 minutes until a toothpick is clean with no wet batter and they are golden brown on top. If making the chocolate chip version, they will be done in around 20 minutes, but with the blueberries, it may take a few minutes longer. Cool completely before serving. These are best completely cooled since they still cook as they sit.

. . . .

Nutrition per muffin: 157 calories | 1.7g fat | 3.1g protein | 33.3g carbs | 2.1g fiber | 18g sugar | 233mg sodium

. . . .

PREP: 10 minutes
BAKE: 20 minutes
YIELDS: 10 muffins

. . . .

1¼ cups (160g) gluten-free fine oat flour
¼ cup (40g) brown rice flour
1 tablespoon (15g) baking powder
½ teaspoon (3g) fine salt
½ cup + 2 tablespoons (200g) pure maple syrup
¼ cup + 2 tablespoons (90g) cashew milk or "lite" canned coconut milk, shaken first
¼ cup + 2 tablespoons (90g) dairy-free vanilla yogurt
½ cup (90g) fresh blueberries
3 tablespoons (45g) raw sugar

⇒ tip ⇐

Cashew or "lite" coconut milk works best in these muffins. I advise against soy, which makes them too tough, and light milks, as these are already low-fat muffins and light milks do not do well. If you can't find vanilla yogurt, add 1 teaspoon vanilla extract to the wet ingredients. If you would like to make these with regular all-purpose flour, use 1½ cups (200g) flour in place of the oat and brown rice flours.

PUMPKIN SPICE, CRANBERRY, AND PISTACHIO MORNING COOKIES

PREP: 10 minutes
BAKE: 10 minutes
YIELDS: 13 cookies

. . . .

½ cup (128g) roasted creamy almond butter

6 tablespoons (120g) pure maple syrup

1 tablespoon (8g) ground flaxseed

1 tablespoon (9g) pumpkin pie spice or Pumpkin Pie Spice Blend (page 238)

¼ teaspoon (2g) fine salt

½ cup (50g) gluten-free old-fashioned oats, not instant

½ cup (23g) brown rice crisp cereal

¼ cup (38g) dried cranberries or cherries

¼ cup (38g) unsalted pistachios

This may sound a bit crazy, but I enjoyed these cookies every bit as much as the insanely indulgent cookies from the dessert chapter in this book. That is hard to believe considering chocolate is nowhere in sight. I was moaning happily while eating them. They are wonderfully chewy with a moist and fudgy center and addicting pumpkin spices.

1. Preheat the oven to 350°F (177°C). Line a sheet pan with parchment paper.

2. Add the almond butter, syrup, flaxseed, pumpkin pie spice, and salt to a large bowl, and stir. Add the oats, cereal, cranberries, and pistachios, and stir for a couple of minutes until incorporated and the batter gets very thick and sticky.

3. Using 2 tablespoons worth of batter, roll into tight balls and place them on the prepared pan about 2 inches apart. I fit 9 on one pan. The batter will be very sticky, so wet your fingertips to help, if needed. Do your best to keep the balls pieced together.

4. Use a small square piece of parchment paper to flatten each ball to about ½ inch thick, pushing any loose pieces together. They are fragile at this step but will firm up beautifully as they bake.

5. Bake at 350°F for 10 minutes or until golden brown on top. Leave on the pan to cool for 10 minutes, and then transfer to a wire rack to cool completely. Now, taste one and tell me how freaking delicious they are! Store them in a tight container so they stay moist. They will lose their crispiness by the next day but will still be chewy and delicious.

. . . .

Nutrition per cookie: 132 calories | 7.5g fat | 3.4g protein | 14.5g carbs | 2.2g fiber | 8.8g sugar | 69mg sodium

. . . .

⇝ *tip* ⇜

To make these nut free, sub the almond butter with sunflower seed butter if you don't mind a strong sunflower seed butter taste. Leave out the pistachios or replace with pumpkin seeds.

⫷⫷⫷⫷⇜

SPICE-IS-NICE BAKED OATMEAL SQUARES

These are a cross between baked oatmeal and a granola bar. Baked oatmeal recipes tend to be too mushy for me, but these bars are just right—soft, yet firm. These can be cut and served with fresh fruit and syrup, just like with a traditional oatmeal breakfast. Kids love these! This recipe makes 8 squares that are plenty for a small family for breakfast. However, if you have a large family or want to batch cook, then double the recipe and use an 8-inch square pan.

1. Preheat the oven to 375°F (190°C). Line a 9-x 5-inch loaf pan with parchment paper going in both directions for easy removal later.

2. Add the oats, flaxseed, cinnamon, allspice, ginger, and salt to a large bowl, and stir well. Pour the milk and syrup over the dry ingredients, and stir well. Stir in the pecans, and pour the mixture into the prepared pan.

3. Bake at 375°F for 45 to 50 minutes or until the top is dry and firm. They will have a soft texture but hold together pretty well.

4. Cool for about 15 minutes, and then lift the paper out and place on a cooling rack for another 15 minutes to firm up. Slice into squares. Eat as is, or top with some yogurt, fresh fruit, an extra drizzle of date or maple syrup, and a sprinkle of cinnamon.

Nutrition per square: 214 calories | 9.5g fat | 5g protein | 29.4g carbs | 4.4g fiber | 8g sugar | 130mg sodium

NOTE The only real fat in this recipe is from the coconut milk, which is by far the best choice for moisture, richness, and texture, but if there is an allergy, almond milk or cashew milk will work, too. The coconut milk replaces oil/butter. I highly recommend the Thai Kitchen brand, as it is always smooth and creamy and many brands can be watery. Do not use full-fat, as it is way too thick.

❧ tip ❧

To make these as a quick grab-and-go snack, divide the batter individually among liners in a muffin pan, filling them almost to the top of the liners. Bake at 375°F for 30 to 35 minutes for a soft oatmeal cupcake or closer to 40 minutes for a crunchier top. This idea came from my taste tester, Stacy, who says these have become a huge hit with her children.

PREP: 10 minutes
BAKE: 45 minutes
YIELDS: 8 squares

· · · · · · · · · · · · · · · · · ·

2 cups (200g) gluten-free old-fashioned oats, not instant
2 tablespoons (14g) ground flaxseed
1 tablespoon (8g) ground cinnamon
1½ teaspoons (4g) ground allspice
¾ teaspoon (2g) ground ginger
½ teaspoon (3g) fine salt
1¼ cups (300g) "lite" canned coconut milk, shaken first
5 tablespoons (100g) pure maple syrup
½ cup (60g) chopped pecans

OPTIONAL: fresh fruit, yogurt for serving

SHREDDED WHEAT CINNAMON PECAN CEREAL

PREP: 10 minutes
BAKE: 27 minutes
YIELDS: 6 cups

. . . .

½ cup (160g) pure maple syrup
¼ cup + 2 tablespoons (96g)
   roasted creamy almond butter
3 tablespoons (60g) unsulphured
   molasses
1½ teaspoons (7g) vanilla extract
2½ teaspoons (6g) ground
   cinnamon
¼ teaspoon (2g) fine salt
1½ cups (96g) shredded wheat
   squares
1½ cups (150g) gluten-free
   old-fashioned oats, not instant
½ cup (60g) pecan pieces

Shredded wheat in granola? Yup! I came up with the most amazing way of getting super-crispy granola, and shredded wheat is the trick. It was a total spur-of-the-moment idea when I decided to crush some into my weekly batch of granola to test it out. I was amazed at the crunchy texture. Serve with plant-based milk or with yogurt and fruit. My favorite way to eat this is with almond milk, strawberries, and a glass of orange juice and coffee.

1. Preheat the oven to 325°F (165°C). Line a large sheet pan with parchment paper.

2. Add the syrup, almond butter, molasses, vanilla, cinnamon, and salt to a large bowl, and stir until smooth.

3. Add the shredded wheat squares to a large ziplock bag and pound them to crush into small pieces.

4. Add the shredded wheat, oats, and pecans to the bowl of liquids, and stir well until it's all coated. Spread out the mixture evenly on the prepared pan in a single layer.

5. Bake at 325°F on the center rack for 15 minutes. Remove and stir around the granola very well, making sure to get the bottom of the mixture. Bake 12 more minutes until it is golden brown, watching the edges in the last couple of minutes to make sure they don't burn.

6. Remove from the oven, and cool on the pan for 10 minutes. It will become very crunchy as it cools. Store in a sealed container for up to 2 weeks.

. . . .

Nutrition per cup: 423 calories | 18.2g fat | 8.9g protein | 60g carbs | 7.7g fiber | 25.3g sugar | 140mg sodium

. . . .

tip

To make these nut free, sub the almond butter with sunflower seed butter and the pecans with sunflower or pumpkin seeds. For wheat free, sub the shredded wheat with brown rice puff cereal—no need to crush them. If you aren't a fan of molasses, sub with date syrup or brown rice syrup. I do not suggest replacing with additional maple syrup, as it will make the granola too sweet.

SILKY SMOOTH CHIVE AND DILL CREAM CHEESE

Cream cheese addict here! This is the fifth cream cheese recipe that I've written since becoming vegan. I have four others on my blog, and even though I have a sweet tooth, I love savory cream cheese much more than the sweet ones. This cream cheese is incredibly smooth, creamy, dreamy, and tangy. Be sure to use distilled white vinegar in this recipe instead of apple cider vinegar; it gives it an authentic cream cheese flavor. This is absolutely delicious on bagels but is also great as a dip with crackers!

1. Add the cashew butter, yogurt, vinegar, lemon juice, onion powder, and salt to a food processor, and blend until very smooth. A food processor works *much* better than a blender for this. Scrape the sides down well, and blend again until very smooth and creamy. It will be quite runny at this stage but will firm up a lot in the fridge. The flavor fully develops overnight, too.

2. Add the cream cheese to a storage container, and stir in the chives and dill. Place in the freezer for 30 minutes. This will jump-start the chilling and firm it up quicker without making it icy.

3. Transfer to the fridge to firm up at least 4 hours, or overnight is preferred. It will get firmer the longer it sits in the fridge. The texture should be really smooth, creamy, and light, not excessively firm.

. . . .

Nutrition per ¼ cup: 216 calories | 17g fat | 4g protein | 13.2g carbs | 1.8g fiber | 5g sugar | 242mg sodium

. . . .

NOTE I make my own raw cashew butter for my recipes. (See page 247 for directions about how to make it.) Most store versions have added oils, salt, or sugar and will ruin the flavor and texture of this. It must be raw cashew butter, as roasted will be too strong of a flavor.

PREP: 10 minutes
CHILL: 4½+ hours
YIELDS: 1 cup

. . . .

½ cup (128g) raw cashew butter
½ cup (120g) plain unsweetened coconut yogurt
1 tablespoon (15g) distilled white vinegar
2 teaspoons (10g) fresh lemon juice
¼ teaspoon (1g) onion powder
¼ teaspoon (2g) fine salt
3 tablespoons (9g) finely chopped chives
¾ teaspoon (1g) dried dill

⇥ tip ⇤

For the yogurt, the So Delicious brand of "unsweetened coconut" works best for this. It thickens up best and is very tangy.

⫷⫷⫷⫷

ROASTED POTATO AND VEGGIE HASH

PREP: 20 minutes
COOK: 35 minutes
YIELDS: 4 servings

. . . .

3 cups (375g) peeled, diced sweet potatoes (½-inch pieces)

3 cups (450g) diced Yukon Gold potatoes (½-inch pieces)

1 packed cup (160g) diced red onion

2 red and green bell peppers, diced (350g)

2 tablespoons (30g) fresh lemon juice

1¼ teaspoons (8g) fine salt, separated

½ + ⅛ teaspoon (2.5g) ground black pepper, separated

1 teaspoon (4g) garlic powder

OPTIONAL: 1 tablespoon freshly chopped rosemary or herb of choice for serving; Restaurant-Style Chipotle Salsa (page 104) or store-bought salsa

My absolute favorite food to eat is potatoes, and one of my favorite ways to eat them is a breakfast-style hash. I have learned how to make them oil free and amazing. The trick is how you cook and season them—just add fresh lemon juice and minimal spice and they are perfection. These are not crispy like fries but rather a baked and soft texture. They turn out incredibly moist, juicy, and delicious! They have a peppery kick, so reduce the black pepper to ¼ teaspoon if serving to kids.

1. Preheat the oven to 400°F (200°C). Line a very large sheet pan with parchment paper. This makes a lot, so a large pan is needed.

2. Add the diced sweet potatoes and Yukon Gold potatoes to a large ziplock bag, and set aside.

3. Add the onion and bell peppers to a medium bowl, and set aside.

4. Add the lemon juice, 1 teaspoon salt, ½ teaspoon black pepper, and garlic powder to a small cup, and stir well. Pour the mixture into the bag of potatoes. Shake the bag well, pressing the bag with your hands to ensure the potatoes all get coated well.

5. Spread out the potatoes evenly on the prepared pan in a single layer, making sure they don't overlap. Bake at 400°F for 15 minutes, and remove from the oven.

6. Turn the heat up to 425°F (220°C).

7. For the bowl of bell peppers and onion, make sure they are dry and not sitting in excess moisture at the bottom of the bowl. If they are, drain them and pat well with a paper towel. Season the bell peppers and onion with the remaining ¼ teaspoon salt and the remaining ⅛ teaspoon black pepper, and toss to ensure even coating. Add them to the pan of potatoes, and stir around all the veggies until evenly mixed. Sprinkle lightly on top with salt and pepper.

8. Bake at 425°F for 15 to 20 minutes or until the potatoes are fork-tender and browning nicely. I like to turn up the broiler for the last minute or two to get extra browning. To serve, sprinkle with freshly chopped rosemary or herb of choice, if desired. Serve with salsa. It really livens up these already delicious potatoes.

. . . .

Nutrition per cup: 216 calories | 0.4g fat | 5.1g protein | 50.8g carbs | 7.7g fiber | 10.8g sugar | 822mg sodium

. . . .

NOTE The lemon juice is what helps the seasonings to stick to the potatoes since there is no oil. It also prevents the potatoes from sticking to the parchment paper, so don't replace with water!

SCRUMPTIOUS SNACKS & APPETIZERS

Appetizers and snacks feel interchangeable to me—most can easily go both ways, which is why they're combined here in one chapter. They range from nuts, healthy cookies, and granola to more hearty, impressive, party-time options—you know, the ones you would serve at a Super Bowl party.

I'm sharing a variety here, so no matter how you categorize them, you'll find options that are easy to make, full of flavor, and perfect for any occasion. Creamy Lemon and Garlic White Bean Crostini (on page 63) and Tex-Mex Potato Skins (on page 60), for example, are not only beautiful enough to serve at a party but are sure to tame hungry tummies while amazing guests with just how tasty plant-based dishes truly can be!

ON-THE-GO LEMON-POPPY SEED MUFFINS

PREP: 10 minutes
BAKE: 20 minutes
YIELDS: 12 muffins

. . . .

1 cup (112g) blanched almond flour

1 cup (160g) white rice flour

½ cup (80g) potato starch

1 tablespoon (15g) baking powder

½ teaspoon (3g) fine salt

¾ cup (240g) pure maple syrup

½ cup (120g) cashew milk or canned "lite" coconut milk

3 tablespoons (45g) fresh lemon juice

2 teaspoons (7g) poppy seeds

➤ tip ➤

The almond flour is crucial, as it is what makes the muffins moist since there is no oil. It is important to use white rice flour and not brown here, as the white rice has much stronger binding qualities than brown. Note that potato starch is not the same as potato flour. If you cannot find potato starch, sub with cornstarch. I do not recommend other starches, as they will yield less desirable results.

Perfectly tart, not too sweet, light, fluffy, and incredibly moist. The lemon juice keeps these from being too sweet, making them the perfect on-the-go breakfast or snack. Be sure you use fresh lemon juice; bottled is too sour. There's a lemon glaze included to drizzle on top for a dessert variation, too! I always recommend a scale for baking to ensure accurate results.

1. Preheat the oven to 350°F (177°C). Line a 12-cup muffin pan with parchment paper liners or Reynolds StayBrite baking cups, as neither of these stick at all. Regular paper liners stick bad.

2. Add the almond flour, rice flour, starch, baking powder, and salt to a large bowl, and whisk well. Add the syrup, milk, lemon juice, and poppy seeds, and whisk until smooth. Divide the batter evenly among the prepared muffin cups.

3. Bake at 350°F for 20 to 22 minutes or until a toothpick comes out clean. Let the muffins cool in the pan for 10 minutes, and then transfer them to a wire rack to cool completely. These are best made the day of. Store any leftovers in an airtight container at room temperature or in the fridge for a couple of days to keep them moist.

. . . .

Nutrition per muffin: 188 calories | 5.3g fat | 2.8g protein | 33g carbs | 1.7g fiber | 12.5g sugar | 108mg sodium

. . . .

LEMON GLAZE FOR A DESSERT MUFFIN

Add ½ cup (76g) powdered sugar, 1½ teaspoons (8g) fresh lemon juice, and 1 teaspoon (5g) cashew milk to a small bowl, and whisk until completely smooth. It will seem too dry at first but keep whisking. The muffins need to be cooled before glazing. Once cooled, drop about a teaspoon of the glaze on the center of each muffin and spread around. Don't spread it too far out, as the glaze will naturally spread on its own after a minute. Top with extra poppy seeds. Let the glaze set at room temperature and serve.

SUNFLOWER–CINNAMON SPICE CHIA BALLS

These may not look like much, but they are so incredibly delicious that I practically ate half the batter straight from the food processor. These are the perfect snack to give you a healthy boost of fats from the seeds instead of processed oils. Plus, many of the ingredients offer a nice dose of protein, especially the quinoa flakes. Be sure to use quick-cooking oats here. The old-fashioned variety will be too large and won't bind well. If you like, you can roll the balls in some extra cinnamon, but if that's too much for you, just leave them plain.

1. Add the quinoa flakes, sugar, chia seeds, pumpkin seeds, cinnamon, allspice, salt, and pepper to a food processor, and process just until well mixed. Add the syrup, sunflower seed butter, and 1 tablespoon (15g) water, and pulse until large sticky clumps form and the mixture holds together when pressed with your fingers.

2. Form 1-inch balls with your hands. Store them in the fridge in a sealed container for up to 14 days.

Nutrition per ball: 110 calories | 5.4g fat | 3.3g protein | 12.8g carbs | 2.3g fiber | 5.5g sugar | 50mg sodium

PREP: 15 minutes
YIELDS: 14 balls

1 cup (112g) quinoa flakes or gluten-free quick-cooking oats
2 tablespoons (24g) coconut sugar
2 tablespoons (24g) chia seeds
1 tablespoon (12g) pumpkin seeds
1½ teaspoons (4g) ground cinnamon
¼ teaspoon (1g) ground allspice
⅛ teaspoon fine salt
⅛ teaspoon ground black pepper
3 tablespoons (60g) pure maple syrup
7 tablespoons (112g) sunflower seed butter (such as SunButter)

➤ tip ➤

For sunflower seed butter, I use the SunButter brand that has no added oils and just a small amount of sugar and salt. I prefer the flavor of this brand. If you don't need these to be nut free, peanut butter and cashew butter are delicious subs. I wouldn't recommend almond butter, as it makes the balls too greasy, and they won't hold together as well.

HEALTHY APPLE PIE COOKIES

PREP: 15 minutes
CHILL: 30 minutes
BAKE: 10 minutes
YIELDS: 12 cookies

. . . .

1 cup (100g) gluten-free old-fashioned oats, not instant

1½ teaspoons (3g) ground cinnamon

½ teaspoon (1g) ground allspice

¼ teaspoon ground nutmeg

Pinch of fine salt

1½ cups (43g) freeze-dried apple pieces

1 cup (150g) whole raw almonds or preferred nuts

6 tablespoons (120g) pure maple syrup

5 tablespoons (80g) roasted creamy almond butter

tip

Feel free to sub walnuts or pecans for the almonds, if desired. Those nuts have a higher oil content and will make the batter more moist, so you may not need all the water; start by adding just 1 tablespoon. To make these nut free, sub the almonds with raw sunflower seed kernels and the almond butter with sunflower seed butter. This obviously will yield more of a sunflower seed flavor.

My all-time favorite fruit is apples, and I love cinnamon the most when it comes to desserts, so that's the inspiration for these spiced apple pie cookies. Be sure to use freeze-dried apples and not fresh in this recipe. These are mildly sweet since they are meant to be a snack and not an indulgent cookie—they're especially fabulous as snacks in kids' lunches. Check out the desserts chapter starting on page 190 for truly indulgent cookies!

1. Add the oats, cinnamon, allspice, nutmeg, and salt to a food processor, and pulse a few times to evenly incorporate the spices. Add the dried apple pieces and almonds, and pulse a few times to break them up into smaller pieces but not into a meal. Add the syrup, almond butter, and 2 tablespoons (30g) water, and process until it comes together in sticky, thick clumps. You will need to stop and break up the mixture and press it back down a few times. It is ready when you can press the mixture together and the mixture is no longer dry and crumbly. Place the processor bowl in the fridge for 30 minutes to firm up a bit before rolling into balls.

2. Preheat the oven to 375°F (190°C). Line a sheet pan with parchment paper.

3. Once chilled, scoop 2 tablespoons of the batter into your hands and roll into balls. If it's still too sticky, chill for another 30 minutes. Place the cookies onto the prepared pan spaced a couple of inches apart. You should get 12. Press each cookie down to ½ inch thick.

4. Bake at 375°F for 10 to 15 minutes or until they have a nice golden brown color on top. Bake them less for a chewier texture or longer for a more crisp texture. I bake mine around 12 minutes. Cool them on the pan for 10 minutes, and then transfer to a wire rack to cool completely. They firm up a lot as they cool. Keep any extras sealed in an airtight container or ziplock bag so they don't dry out for up to 3 days.

. . . .

Nutrition per cookie: 147 calories | 7.4g fat | 4g protein | 18.1g carbs | 3g fiber | 8.5g sugar | 18mg sodium

. . . .

oil free • gluten free

CHOCOLATE-CHERRY GRANOLA

Chocolate and dried cherries are a magical flavor combination. The tart-sweet cherries are a perfect balance for the rich chocolate. I intentionally made this granola only mildly sweet. If you'd like a sweeter granola, increase the maple syrup to ¾ cup. Enjoy it as is or over yogurt, cereal, or even ice cream. I love to store this granola in individual ziplock bags for on-the-go snacks while I'm out running errands. This is great for snacks for kids' lunches as well.

1. Preheat the oven to 325°F (165°C). Line a large sheet pan with parchment paper.

2. Add the syrup, almond butter, and salt to a large bowl, and stir well until smooth. Add the remaining ingredients, and stir until everything is well coated and wet. Spread the oats mixture out evenly in a single layer onto the prepared pan.

3. Bake at 325°F on the lowest rack for 15 minutes, stir the granola around well so the bottom cooks evenly, and bake 10 to 15 more minutes or until done. Watch the edges closely in the last couple of minutes so they don't burn. The granola will feel soft upon removal from the oven but will crisp up as it cools. Let cool on the pan for 15 minutes. Store in a sealed container for up to 2 weeks.

. . . .

Nutrition per ¼ cup: 281 calories | 8.6g fat | 7.7g protein | 47.5g carbs | 6.1g fiber | 15.6g sugar | 80mg sodium

. . . .

NOTE Use the nut butter or seed butter of your choice in this granola. To make this nut free, make sure to use seeds instead of nuts. I used raw sunflower kernels.

PREP: 5 minutes
BAKE: 25 minutes
YIELDS: 2 cups

. . . .

½ cup + 2 tablespoons (200g) pure maple syrup
¼ cup + 2 tablespoons (96g) roasted creamy almond butter
¼ teaspoon (2g) fine salt
3 cups (280g) gluten-free old-fashioned oats, not instant
5 tablespoons (30g) unsweetened natural cocoa powder
½ cup (75g) preferred seeds or nuts
½ cup (75g) dried cherries

TEX-MEX POTATO SKINS

PREP: 20 minutes
COOK: 1 hour, 15 minutes
YIELDS: 8 servings

. . . .

4 large russet potatoes (1,800g)
1 large red bell pepper (145g),
 finely diced
1 teaspoon (6g) fine salt,
 separated
¼ + ⅛ teaspoon (1.5g) ground
 black pepper, separated
1 (15-ounce) can low-sodium black
 beans, drained and rinsed, or
 1½ cups cooked (255g)
¼ teaspoon (1g) ground cumin
1½ cups (225g) frozen sweet corn
½ cup (76g) jalapeño slices from
 a jar, chopped
1 large avocado (170g)
½ tablespoon (8g) fresh lime juice

These potato skins are unbelievably delicious and simple. Serve them at your next gathering or party—or just make them for yourself. I cook the black beans and corn separately to maintain the vibrant color of each ingredient—it makes the potato skins prettier. If you're not worried about that, you can heat them all together in one pot. Use the leftover potato to make mashed potatoes.

1. Preheat the oven to 425°F (220°C). Line a sheet pan with foil.

2. Place the potatoes on the prepared pan; bake at 425°F for 45 to 60 minutes or until very tender. You will know they are done when you can slightly squeeze them and they give a little. The baking time will vary depending on the size.

3. Add the bell pepper to a small sheet pan lined with parchment paper, and season with ¼ teaspoon of the salt and ⅛ teaspoon of the pepper. Set aside.

4. Add the beans, cumin, ½ teaspoon salt, and remaining ¼ teaspoon pepper to a small pot, and stir well. Set aside. Add the corn to a separate small pot. Set aside.

5. Once the potatoes are done baking, cool them for 10 minutes. Then slice them in half lengthwise. Use a spoon to scoop out the flesh of the potatoes, leaving about ¼ inch remaining along the edges and bottom. Flip the potato shells over and lightly spray the skin sides with nonstick spray and season with the remaining ¼ teaspoon salt or more to taste. If you avoid oil, you can skip the spray, but I found it to make them extra crispy and flavorful.

6. Increase the oven temperature to 450°F (230°C). Line the same pan with parchment paper, and place the cut potatoes cut sides down. Bake at 450°F for about 10 minutes or until the skins are very crispy. If you didn't use oil, they take a few minutes longer to get crispy. At the same time, place the pan of bell peppers on the bottom rack below the potatoes. Both the potatoes and bell peppers should be done at about the same time. The bell peppers should be beginning to char along the edges.

7. When the potatoes and bell peppers have just a couple of minutes left, heat up the beans and corn.

8. Fill each potato with beans, corn, and bell peppers and stir the mixture around a bit. Top with chopped jalapeños.

9. Peel and mash the avocado in a bowl, and add the lime juice. Mash repeatedly until completely smooth. Add to a ziplock bag, cut off a tiny corner, and drizzle on top of each potato. Season the tops with an extra sprinkling of salt and black pepper, if desired.

. . . .

Nutrition per serving: 279 calories | 5.5g fat | 7.6g protein | 53.1g carbs | 9.8g fiber | 5.5g sugar | 514mg sodium

. . . .

CREAMY LEMON AND GARLIC WHITE BEAN CROSTINI

This is the perfect fancy appetizer for entertaining or bringing to a party. Even better, they are so simple to make. They also pack quite the protein punch.

1. Add the milk to a small bowl; whisk in the flour until smooth. Set aside.

2. Preheat the oven to 400°F (200°C). Line a sheet pan with foil.

3. Add the garlic and 3 tablespoons (45g) water to a medium pot over medium heat. Bring to a simmer, and cook for about 3 minutes or until softened, stirring often. Add the milk mixture, Worcestershire, salt, pepper, and beans. Stir well, and bring to a simmer. Reduce the heat to medium-low, and cook for about 5 minutes or until thickened. Add the spinach and lemon juice, and heat through for 1 to 2 minutes or until the spinach is wilted. Taste and add more spices, if desired. Let the mixture cool a few minutes while toasting the bread. It will get thicker as it cools.

4. Add the sliced baguette to the prepared pan, and bake at 400°F for 5 to 10 minutes or until toasty brown.

5. Spoon 2 to 3 tablespoons of the bean mixture onto each toast. Top with red pepper flakes, if desired. Serve immediately.

. . . .
Nutrition per 2 slices: 243 calories | 2.6g fat | 10.7g protein | 44.8g carbs | 4.3g fiber | 2.7g sugar | 598mg sodium
. . . .

NOTE This recipe relies on a good amount of milk, so be selective when choosing your milk, as the flavor will definitely be pronounced in the end result. I do not recommend cashew or almond, as they didn't taste good in my trials. I recommend soy or canned "lite" coconut milk, shaken well first before measuring. If you're not gluten free, you can sub all-purpose flour for the brown rice flour.

PREP: 10 minutes
COOK: 18 minutes
YIELDS: 16 toasts

. . . .

1 cup (240g) soy milk or other creamy milk

2 tablespoons (20g) brown rice flour

5 large garlic cloves, minced (15g)

1 tablespoon (15g) vegan Worcestershire

½ teaspoon (3g) fine salt

¼ teaspoon (1g) ground black pepper

2 (15-ounce) cans low-sodium cannellini beans, drained and rinsed, or 3 cups cooked (510g)

1½ packed cups roughly chopped fresh spinach (60g)

2 tablespoons (30g) fresh lemon juice

1 (15-ounce) French bread baguette, sliced ¼ inch thick

OPTIONAL: red pepper flakes

SMOKY ANCHO CHILE ROASTED ALMONDS

PREP: 5 minutes
COOK: 10 minutes
YIELDS: 2 cups

. . . .

1 tablespoon (20g) pure maple
    syrup
½ teaspoon (1g) smoked paprika
½ teaspoon (2g) onion powder
½ teaspoon (3g) fine salt
¼ teaspoon (1g) garlic powder
¼ teaspoon ancho chile pepper
    powder
2 cups (320g) whole raw, unsalted
    almonds

A little smoky, a little salty, a little sweet—these are so flavorful that you'll never need to buy roasted almonds again.

1. Preheat the oven to 350°F (177°C). Line a sheet pan with parchment paper.

2. Add the syrup, paprika, onion powder, salt, garlic powder, and chile pepper powder to a large bowl, and stir until well mixed. Add the almonds, stirring until well coated. Spread the almonds out evenly onto the prepared pan, making sure not to overlap them.

3. Bake at 350°F for 5 minutes. Stir them around well and flatten out the layer so they are not overlapping. Bake 5 to 7 more minutes. Watch them carefully at the end to ensure they don't burn. They will be sticky upon removal from the oven but will dry up as they cool. Cool 15 minutes on the pan, and then break them up to keep them from sticking to each other. If they are still slightly sticky, bake for another 1 to 2 minutes and that should do it. Store in a ziplock bag or an airtight container for up to 2 weeks.

. . . .

Nutrition per ¼ cup: 239 calories | 20g fat | 8.5g protein | 10.5g carbs | 5.1g fiber | 3.3g sugar | 118mg sodium

. . . .

❧ *tip* ❧

If you are not a fan of the spices used on the almonds,
then you can omit them and just use the salt and syrup for a sweet
almond variety. Kids will likely prefer the version without the spices.

❧ 4 ❧

TIME-CRUNCH LUNCHES

What do you do when you are craving a healthy lunch but don't have much time to prepare it? Well, I have the answer. This chapter contains an assortment of tasty recipes that are ready in 30 minutes or less from start to finish. With a handful of the right ingredients and a little bit of time, you can eat healthy and enjoy something fresh for lunch every day if you like. We all have enough challenges in our day, so no need to make lunch complicated, right? While I, of course, love each recipe, my favorites are the Pizza Quesadillas on page 83 and The Perfect Pasta Salad on page 76. Those were gigantic hits with my taste testers, and I hope you love them, too!

20-MINUTE ALFREDO

PREP: 5 minutes
COOK: 15 minutes
YIELDS: 4 servings

. . . .

For the pasta
14 ounces fettuccine, linguine, or preferred pasta

½ tablespoon (9g) fine salt

For the Alfredo sauce
2 cups (480g) low-sodium vegetable broth

¼ cup (64g) raw cashew butter or a heaping ½ cup (64g) raw, unsalted cashews

2 teaspoons (10g) apple cider vinegar

1 to 2 tablespoons (8 to 16g) nutritional yeast

2 tablespoons (20g) brown rice flour or all-purpose flour

1 teaspoon (3g) garlic powder

1 teaspoon (1g) Italian seasoning

1 teaspoon (6g) fine salt

¼ teaspoon (1g) ground black pepper

OPTIONAL: peas, carrots, broccoli, or any vegetables you like

Meet the most popular pasta recipe from my blog. Well, it's kind of tied with my original garlic Alfredo version, but this one is faster and creamier and so much like dairy. It has become a staple in many of my readers' homes. I hope you love it, too.

1. Add 12 cups (2,880g) very hot water to a large pot, cover, and bring to a boil. Add the pasta and salt, and quickly stir around. Boil for 7 to 9 minutes or until al dente. (Your cook times may vary depending on the pasta you use.)

2. While waiting on the water to boil, make the sauce. Add the broth, cashew butter, vinegar, yeast, flour, garlic powder, Italian seasoning, salt, and pepper to a high-powered blender or food processor (see Note); blend until very smooth, scraping the sides as needed. It will be very runny.

3. Add the sauce to a large pan over high heat. Once it starts simmering all over, immediately turn down the heat to medium-low, and whisk continuously for about 3 minutes until thickened. Don't walk away from it, as the sauce will get lumpy if you overcook it. You want it to be smooth but not overly thick. It will thicken even more as it cools. Remove from the heat, and cover.

4. Drain the pasta, and divide among the plates. Add the sauce. Taste and add more salt or pepper, if desired. Add in any veggies, if desired.

. . . .

Nutrition per serving: 491 calories | 10.1g fat | 16.4g protein | 85.5g carbs | 4.2g fiber | 5.6g sugar | 988mg sodium

. . . .

NOTE To make this gluten free, use your preferred gluten-free pasta. Note that gluten-free pasta cooks faster and gets mushy easily, and I'd suggest rinsing it once cooked since it can get rather sticky. If you are using whole cashews (instead of cashew butter) and do not have a high-powered blender like a Vitamix, you'll need to soak your cashews for 8 hours or preferably overnight in a bowl of warm water to soften, and then drain, rinse, and proceed with the recipe. Otherwise, the sauce will be gritty. If using soaked cashews, a food processor works better than a regular, non-high-powered blender. For the nutritional yeast, it's important to use a non-fortified brand, as some can leave a strong vitamin taste. I like Sari or Dr. Fuhrman's. If you avoid yeast, simply omit it and increase the salt a bit, to taste. If you cannot find the Italian seasoning, you can sub with ¼ teaspoon each of dried oregano, thyme, basil, and rosemary.

EASY ONE-PAN RED CURRY WITH SPINACH AND CARROTS

I love this curry for when I need something quick, easy, and yet still full of wonderful flavor. This curry is comfort in a bowl, and the one-pan method makes it simple. This dish comes together quickly, so be sure to have all of your ingredients prepped and ready to go before you start. You can serve this over rice, if you like, to soak up even more of the sauce. The cashews provide a lovely crunch to this dish, but you can omit them to make it nut free.

1. Add the carrots, ginger, and ½ cup (120g) water to a large pan over medium-low heat. Cook for 5 to 8 minutes, stirring occasionally, until the carrots are almost fully tender. Add more water if necessary, 1 tablespoon at a time, to keep the carrots cooking. Add the chickpeas, milk, curry paste, salt, and sugar, and stir well.

2. Increase the heat to high, and bring to a boil. Once boiling, cover and reduce the heat to low, and simmer for about 5 minutes or until the chickpeas and carrots are tender and the sauce has slightly thickened. Stir in the spinach and lime juice, and remove the pan from the heat, stirring until the spinach is wilted. Taste and add any extra lime juice or salt, if desired. Garnish with crushed red pepper for added heat and cashews for a satisfying crunch, if desired.

. . . .

Nutrition per serving: 400 calories | 24.3g fat | 12.3g protein | 37.8g carbs | 10.7g fiber | 8.4g sugar | 982mg sodium

. . . .

PREP: 15 minutes
COOK: 10 minutes
YIELDS: 4 servings

. . . .

3 medium carrots, cut into ¼-inch rounds (105g)

1-inch knob fresh ginger, peeled and grated (12g)

2 (13.5-ounce) cans low-sodium chickpeas, drained and rinsed, or 3 cups cooked (510g)

1 (13.5-ounce) can full-fat coconut milk

¼ cup (60g) red curry paste

½ teaspoon (3g) fine salt

1 tablespoon (12g) coconut sugar

3 packed cups (84g) fresh spinach leaves

1 tablespoon (15g) fresh lime juice

OPTIONAL: cashews and crushed red pepper for garnish

OIL-FREE PEANUT-VEGGIE STIR-FRY

PREP: 20 minutes
COOK: 10 minutes
YIELDS: 4 servings

. . . .

8 ounces skinny vermicelli rice noodles

5 tablespoons (80g) peanut butter or sunflower seed butter (such as SunButter)

3 tablespoons (45g) gluten-free low-sodium soy sauce or tamari

1 tablespoon (15g) fresh lime juice

2½ tablespoons (25g) coconut sugar

2 medium carrots, peeled and sliced into ¼- x 3-inch sticks (130g)

½ tablespoon (8g) minced fresh ginger

¼ teaspoon (2g) fine salt

2 large bell peppers, sliced into skinny strips (274g)

OPTIONAL: ½ cup (55g) chopped fresh green onions, toasted sesame seeds, red pepper flakes for garnish

❧ tip ❧

To make this nut free, sub sunflower seed butter for the peanut butter in this recipe.

This stir-fry is every bit as satisfying as the ones cooked in oil. The key is the right pan (a wok or nonstick pan, not stainless steel) and cooking method so the veggies don't stick. This stir-fry cooks very quickly, so you will need to have everything ready to go before you start. Use any color combination of bell peppers you like, and serve the stir-fry over white rice instead of rice noodles, if you prefer. A word of caution: The peanut sauce is addictive. It may cause you to put this dish on repeat!

1. Bring 8 cups (1,920g) water to a boil in a large pot. Add the noodles and immediately remove from the heat. Let the noodles sit in the hot water for about 3 minutes. They should be tender but still firm. Drain, and set aside.

2. While waiting on the water to boil, make the sauce. Add the peanut butter, soy sauce, lime juice, coconut sugar, and 3 tablespoons (45g) water to a small bowl, and whisk until completely smooth. Set aside.

3. Add ½ cup (120g) water to a large wok or nonstick pan. Turn the heat to medium-high. Once the water comes to a gentle boil, add the carrots, ginger, and salt to the pan. Stir constantly for 5 minutes until the carrots are beginning to get tender but are still crisp. Add the bell peppers and an additional 2 tablespoons (30g) water, and cook for 3 minutes, stirring constantly, until the bell peppers are crisp-tender. (If you prefer your vegetables to be more tender, add a bit more water and cook to the desired tenderness.) Add the peanut sauce, and cook for just about 30 seconds or so, just until the veggies are coated and the sauce takes on a slightly creamy texture. It will happen quickly. Don't overcook the sauce or it will no longer be creamy and will just stick to the pan. Taste and add more soy sauce for more saltiness and more lime juice for more tang, if desired. Serve over the rice noodles. Garnish with the green onions, sesame seeds, and red pepper flakes to really punch up the crunch and flavor, if desired.

. . . .

Nutrition per serving: 389 calories | 1.4g fat | 5.4g protein | 67.5g carbs | 3.8g fiber | 11.4g sugar | 678mg sodium

. . . .

MEXICAN TAHINI CHICKPEAS

This is the perfect recipe to make for a really quick lunch. These chickpeas are loaded with protein and are super filling. They are tasty on their own, but they can also be used as a filling in lettuce wraps, sandwiches, tacos, or burritos—my favorite way to eat them is on toasted bread with lettuce, green onions, and tomatoes. The tahini sauce is also great as a dipping sauce for burritos or roasted potatoes.

1. Add the tahini, lime juice, syrup, onion powder, garlic powder, chili powder, cumin, salt, and 2 tablespoons (30g) water to a bowl, and whisk until completely smooth. Taste and add more salt or lime juice, if desired. This makes ¾ cup of sauce. Reserve ½ cup of the sauce for the chickpeas, and reserve the remaining ¼ cup for another use, such as for drizzling on tacos or as a dipping sauce.

2. Add the reserved ½ cup tahini sauce to the chickpeas, and mash with a fork until the mixture is thick and chunky and has a cohesive texture.

Nutrition per serving: 274 calories | 13.6g fat | 11g protein | 30.7g carbs | 7.8g fiber | 7.6g sugar | 408mg sodium

⇢ *tip* ⇠

If you are not a fan of the strong, bitter taste of tahini, then you can sub with roasted almond butter or cashew butter. The syrup helps balance out the bitterness of the tahini, but the finished sauce does taste like tahini.

PREP: 10 minutes
YIELDS: 3 servings

. . . .

6 tablespoons (84g) runny roasted tahini
¼ cup (60g) fresh lime juice
4 teaspoons (28g) pure maple syrup
2 teaspoons (6g) onion powder
2 teaspoons (6g) garlic powder
2 teaspoons (6g) chili powder
2 teaspoons (6g) ground cumin
½ teaspoon (3g) fine salt
1 (15-ounce) can low-sodium chickpeas, drained and rinsed, or 1½ cups cooked (255g)

OPTIONAL: sandwich bread or corn tortillas, lettuce, chopped red or green onions, chopped tomatoes for serving

THE PERFECT PASTA SALAD

PREP: 15 minutes
COOK: 10 minutes
YIELDS: 4 servings

. . . .

6 tablespoons (90g) low-sodium
    vegetable broth
3 tablespoons (45g) red wine
    vinegar
1 teaspoon (1g) dried oregano
⅛ teaspoon ground black
    pepper
8 ounces fusilli pasta
¾ cup (108g) sliced black olives
¾ cup (113g) frozen sweet corn
¾ cup (100g) halved cherry
    tomatoes
½ loosely packed cup (12g)
    chopped fresh basil

This is easily one of my favorite recipes. It is salty from the olives, sweet from the corn, sour from the red wine vinegar, and tangy from the tomatoes. The oregano and fresh basil bring it all together. And surprise, the vinaigrette has zero oil, and you know what, it doesn't need it! You can add the frozen corn straight to this dish, as it helps chill the pasta instantly. To make this gluten free, sub your favorite gluten-free pasta.

1. Combine the broth, vinegar, oregano, and pepper in small bowl, whisking until combined. Set aside in the fridge to chill.

2. Bring a large pot of water (about 8 cups, 1,920g) to a boil. Add the pasta, and cook 10 minutes or until al dente. Drain and rinse the pasta in very cold water. This will jump-start chilling the pasta salad. Transfer the pasta to a large bowl. Add the olives, corn, tomatoes, and basil, and stir to combine.

3. Pour in the vinaigrette, starting with ¼ cup and increasing until it reaches the flavor you want. Keep in mind that the flavors will relax a bit overnight in the fridge, so you will likely add the remaining vinaigrette the next day if you don't use it all now. Toss to coat everything well. Taste and add salt and more pepper, if desired. The frozen corn does chill the salad nicely right away and it can be eaten immediately, but I prefer to chill the salad in the fridge for a couple of hours before serving.

. . . .
Nutrition per serving: 279 calories | 4.2g fat | 9.5g protein | 53.4g carbs | 4.6g fiber | 3.5g sugar | 250mg sodium
. . . .

SOUTHWEST LIME SALAD

This salad—a reader favorite on my blog—may use basic ingredients, but it packs a punch of flavor. It can be served either warm or chilled. The crushed tortilla chips add a nice crunch, but you can omit them if you want to keep this recipe gluten free. This salad is also yummy as a filling for tacos.

1. Preheat the oven to 400°F (200°C). Line a sheet pan with parchment paper.

2. Place the chopped bell pepper on the prepared pan, and season to taste with salt and pepper. Roast at 400°F for 10 minutes.

3. While the peppers are roasting, place the corn and beans in separate bowls, and warm up either in the microwave or on the stovetop.

4. Combine the lime juice, syrup, chili powder, cumin, and salt in a small bowl, and whisk well. Add the lime mixture to a small pan over medium-low heat. Cook for 2 to 3 minutes to heat through.

5. Add the roasted bell pepper to a large serving bowl. Add the corn, beans, and lime mixture, and toss to coat everything evenly. Taste and add more salt and seasonings, if desired. Add the avocado right before serving, and top with crushed tortilla chips, if desired.

. . . .

Nutrition per serving: 344 calories | 8.5g fat | 15.7g protein | 56g carbs | 20.1g fiber | 7.2g sugar | 374mg sodium

. . . .

PREP: 15 minutes
COOK: 15 minutes
YIELDS: 4 servings

. . . .

2 cups (200g) diced red bell pepper

1¼ cups (168g) frozen sweet corn

2 (15-ounce) cans low-sodium black beans, drained and rinsed, or 3 cups cooked (510g)

¼ cup (60g) fresh lime juice

1 tablespoon (20g) pure maple syrup

1 teaspoon (2.5g) chili powder

½ teaspoon (1.5g) ground cumin

⅛ teaspoon fine salt

1 medium avocado (150g), chopped

OPTIONAL: crushed tortilla chips for serving

ELEVATED AVOCADO TOAST

PREP: 15 minutes
COOK: 10 minutes
YIELDS: 4 toasts

. . . .

2 red bell peppers, cut into
¼-inch strips (274g)
1 medium avocado (150g)
3 packed cups (90g) fresh spinach
2 tablespoons (30g) fresh lemon
juice
½ teaspoon (3g) fine salt
¼ teaspoon (1g) garlic powder
¼ teaspoon (1g) ground black
pepper
1 (15-ounce) can low-sodium
chickpeas, drained and rinsed,
or 1½ cups cooked (255g)
4 slices bread (184g), toasted
¼ cup (60g) jarred jalapeño
slices

❧ tip ❧

The jalapeños give these toasts
an *amazing* flavor, but they may
be a bit strong for kids. Sub fresh
green onions for a milder option.

Avocado toast has pretty much taken over the Internet, and for good
reason—it's healthy and tasty. For this version, I wanted to take the typical
avocado-only variety to the next level, so I created this avocado-chickpea-
spinach mash and topped it with roasted bell peppers for some smokiness
and jalapeños for a kick that's sure to wake you up. For the bell peppers,
a mix of red, orange, and yellow peppers is delicious and pretty.

1. Preheat the oven to 425°F (220°C). Line a sheet pan with parchment paper.

2. Place the bell pepper strips on the prepared pan, and season to taste with salt
and pepper. Roast at 425°F for 10 minutes or until beginning to char on the tips.

3. While the bell peppers are roasting, add the avocado, spinach, lemon juice,
salt, garlic powder, and pepper to a food processor; process until smooth. You
will have to push the spinach down a couple of times to incorporate it. Transfer
the avocado mixture to a large bowl.

4. Add the chickpeas to the avocado mixture, and mash them into the avocado
mixture until well mixed and smooth, creating a lovely thick texture. Make sure
all of the chickpeas are mashed and no longer whole. Taste and add more salt
or pepper, if desired.

5. Divide the avocado mixture among the bread slices. Top with the roasted
bell peppers and jalapeño slices.

. . . .

Nutrition per serving: 289 calories | 8.4g fat | 13.2g protein | 42.3g carbs | 11.7g fiber |
8.6g sugar | 719mg sodium

. . . .

PIZZA QUESADILLAS

I love pizza and I love quesadillas, so combining them creates a glorious result! These truly will remind you of pizza! While this recipe can be made in 30 minutes, to make the process faster and easier, make the cheese sauce and pizza sauce the day before. The cheese sauce thickens nicely overnight.

PREP: 10 minutes
COOK: 10 minutes
YIELDS: 6 servings

1. Add the mashed potatoes, milk, vinegar, and salt to a food processor; process for 2 to 3 minutes or until 100% smooth. A food processor is a must here, as a blender will over-process the cheese and turn it into a sauce and it won't bake up properly. Scrape the sides, and process once more until the sauce gets thick and a bit glue-y and stretchy. Keep in mind, this is not meant to be a cheese replicate on its own but is designed to be baked into these quesadillas or other dishes, if you like. It has a slight potato mouthfeel but works amazingly well in the baked end result. Let the cheese sit to thicken a bit, while gathering the remaining ingredients. If the cheese is runnier than you'd like, add a bit more cooked potato and blend again. Soy milk thickens best; other milks make the texture too runny.

2. Preheat oven to 425°F (220°C). Line 3 large sheet pans with parchment paper.

3. Place 2 tortillas on the prepared pan. Spread 4 to 5 tablespoons of the cheese sauce onto each tortilla, leaving about a ½-inch edge on the outside (so the cheese doesn't ooze all out when baking). Top the cheese with about 3 tablespoons of pizza sauce. Top evenly with olives, basil leaves, and, if desired, red pepper flakes. Top each with a tortilla and gently press down.

4. Bake at 425°F for 8 to 10 minutes until crispy and golden brown around the edges. Remove from the oven, gently press the top of the tortilla and hold for a few seconds (to help it stick). Let the quesadillas sit for 5 to 10 minutes to cool. This will also allow the cheese sauce to firm up a bit before slicing so it doesn't ooze out. Slice with a pizza cutter. Repeat with the remaining tortillas.

Nutrition per serving: 343 calories | 8.5g fat | 10.9g protein | 58.6g carbs | 3.5g fiber | 5.5g sugar | 1,702mg sodium

NOTE Yukon gold potatoes provide the best taste and texture, as well as being stretchy, so don't sub with russet potatoes or the cheese will be less superior. Please bake or microwave the potato instead of boiling, as too much water added to the potato will make the cheese too runny. See page 96 for my microwave instructions. For the best texture and flavor, avoid almond or non-creamy milks. Distilled white vinegar is key to the cheesy flavor, so don't be tempted to sub with apple cider vinegar. If you're making my homemade pizza sauce, omit the red pepper flakes listed in that recipe so the quesadillas aren't too spicy. You can always add some red pepper flakes to the quesadilla, to taste.

For the cheese sauce
1 packed cup (240g) cooked, peeled, mashed Yukon Gold potatoes
1 cup (240g) creamy soy milk or "lite" coconut milk
4 teaspoons (20g) distilled white vinegar
1 teaspcon (6g) fine salt

Remaining ingredients
12 (8-inch) soft flour tortillas
1 cup (240g) Easiest-Ever Pizza/ Spaghetti Sauce (page 230) or store-bought
1 ½ cups (216g) sliced black olives
1 packed cup (30g) fresh basil leaves
OPTIONAL: red pepper flakes

❧ tip ❧

For a richer variation (and if you're not allergic to nuts), a couple of tablespoons of raw cashew butter added to the processor with the other cheese sauce ingredients is a yummy addition!

❮❮❮❮❮

LAZY RED LENTIL–SALSA SOUP

PREP: 10 minutes
COOK: 10 minutes
YIELDS: 4 servings

. . . .

1¼ cups (260g) dry red lentils,
   rinsed well with cold water
½ packed cup (80g) diced red bell
   pepper
1¼ cups (300g) smooth salsa
1 tablespoon (8g) mild chili powder
   or DIY Homemade Chili
   Powder (page 245)
1 tablespoon (2g) dried oregano
1 teaspoon (2g) smoked paprika
¼ teaspoon (1g) ground black
   pepper
¾ cup (105g) frozen sweet corn
1 large avocado (170g), sliced

OPTIONAL: fresh lime juice,
   fresh cilantro for garnish

If you love salsa like I do but are feeling too lazy to chop a lot of veggies, this soup is for you. It's also ideal when you're pressed for time but don't want to settle for a boring, bland meal. Just throw everything into one pot, and you will have a tasty soup to eat in no time. For the salsa, choose one with your preferred heat level and a smooth texture. I use medium and really love Pace Picante here.

1. Add 4 cups (960g) water, lentils, bell pepper, salsa, chili powder, oregano, paprika, and black pepper to a large pot, and stir well until mixed thoroughly. Bring to a boil over high heat. Once boiling, immediately reduce the heat to low, cover with a lid slightly tilted to allow some steam to escape, and simmer for 10 to 15 minutes or just until the lentils are tender. These cook rather fast, so set the timer.

2. Stir in the corn, and heat through for a couple of minutes. Taste and add salt or more salsa, if desired. Depending on the salsa you used, it may need salt. Add a squeeze of lime juice and cilantro for an extra punch of flavor, if desired. Ladle into bowls and top with sliced avocado. For a pretty presentation, adding extra cilantro and lime juice is a lovely touch for serving to guests.

. . . .

Nutrition per serving: 393 calories | 10g fat | 19g protein | 61.2g carbs | 27.8g fiber | 8.9g sugar | 613mg sodium

. . . .

❧ tip ❧

Make sure you are using a standard American chili powder,
which is a blend of different spices (see page 16 for more about why).
If you cannot find one, then make my DIY blend on page 245.

❮❮❮❮

❧ 5 ❧

SAUCES & DRESSINGS

If you follow my blog, then you know I have a thing for creating sauces and dressings. They are what complete many meals, and having a variety helps prevent dishes from becoming boring. If you aren't feeling the same old sauce, switch it up. A new-to-you drizzle on your favorite recipes can truly feel like you are having a different meal each day.

My goal with this chapter is to offer a range of flavorful sauces and dressings so that you are guaranteed to never have bland food. A happy little bonus is that each of these decadent sauces is oil free, too. I hope you love this chapter as much as I do!

THAI PEANUT-SESAME SAUCE

PREP: 10 minutes
YIELDS: heaping 1 cup

· · · · · · · · · · · · · · · · ·

½ cup (128g) creamy natural
    peanut butter
3 tablespoons (45g) gluten-free
    low-sodium soy sauce or tamari
3 tablespoons (60g) agave syrup
2 tablespoons (30g) water
1½ tablespoons (23g) fresh lime
    juice
¾ teaspoon (3g) garlic powder
½ teaspoon (1g) red pepper
    flakes
1- to 2-inch knob (10 to 20g)
    fresh ginger, peeled and
    finely grated
½ tablespoon (4g) toasted
    sesame seeds

When you have the strong desire to eat a sauce with a spoon, then you know you have a good one on your hands. I love bold flavors, and this sauce delivers just that. It is rich in peanut flavor and warm from fresh ginger. It is balanced out with a salty bite from the soy sauce, sweetness from agave, and a touch of tart from fresh lime juice. I suggest making this a day ahead of time, as the flavors really develop beautifully overnight. Also, I suggest freezing your peeled ginger. It will make for easier grating. You can serve this sauce with rice or pasta and veggies. It also makes a fantastic salad dressing.

Add all of the ingredients except the sesame seeds to a food processor, and blend until smooth. This sauce will be creamy and thick. If you prefer it thinner, add more water. Stir in the sesame seeds. Use immediately or store in the fridge for about a week. The sauce will thicken a lot in the fridge because of the peanut butter, so let it sit out at room temperature for 10 to 15 minutes before you're ready to use it. The sauce can be frozen for up to 6 months as well. Just let it thaw overnight in the fridge.

· · · · · · · · · · ·

Nutrition per about 2 tablespoons: 139 calories | 8.3g fat | 4.1g protein | 10.2g carbs | 1.2g fiber | 5.9g sugar | 269mg sodium

· · · · · · · · · · · ·

❧ tip ❧

If you don't have agave on hand, you can sub with maple syrup.
Keep in mind it will yield somewhat of a maple flavor,
which is why I use agave.

CREAMY CAJUN LEMON SAUCE

This creamy sauce has a spicy kick to it, making it the star of anything you add it to. It is great with fritters, vegan "crab cakes," fries, roasted potatoes, salads, or anything you want to liven up! I even love to just dip veggies in it.

1. Add the cashews, ½ cup (120g) water, lemon juice, 1 teaspoon capers, 1 teaspoon thyme, Cajun Spice Seasoning, garlic powder, cayenne pepper, and salt to a high-powered blender or food processor (see Note), and blend until completely smooth. Scrape the sides and blend again. You want it completely smooth. Taste and add more cayenne or salt, if desired.

2. Pour the mixture into a bowl, and stir in the remaining 1 teaspoon thyme and remaining 2 teaspoons capers. Use immediately or store in the fridge for 1 week. The sauce will thicken a lot in the fridge, so let it sit out at room temperature for 15 minutes or so to return it to the original texture. Or freeze for 6 months. Thaw overnight in the fridge.

. . . .

Nutrition per 2 tablespoons: 85 calories | 6.6g fat | 2.8g protein | 5.1g carbs | 0.6g fiber | 1g sugar | 138mg sodium

. . . .

NOTE If you do not have a high-powered blender like a Vitamix, you'll need to soak your cashews for 8 hours or preferably overnight in a bowl of warm water to soften, and then drain, rinse, and proceed with the recipe. Otherwise, the dressing will be gritty. If using soaked cashews, a food processor works better than a regular, non-high-powered blender. Alternatively, you can sub with raw cashew butter (see page 247 for how to make this) for the same amount, 150g, which is about 9 heaping tablespoons. You can use store-bought Cajun seasoning. Just make sure to omit the salt called for in the recipe if your blend has added salt.

PREP: 5 minutes
YIELDS: 1¼ cups

. . . .

1 cup (150g) raw, unsalted cashews

½ cup (120g) water

3 tablespoons (45g) fresh lemon juice

3 teaspoons (12g) capers, separated

2 teaspoons (2g) dried thyme, separated

1 teaspoon (2g) Cajun Spice Seasoning (page 241)

¼ teaspoon (1g) garlic powder

⅛ to ¼ teaspoon (0.5 to 1g) cayenne pepper

½ teaspoon (3g) fine salt

❧ *tip* ❧

For a nut-free version, sub the cashews with the same amount of cannellini beans if you don't mind bean-based sauces. Another option is to sub with ½ packed cup (120g) cooked, peeled, and mashed Yukon Gold potato. The potato thickens much more than cashews, which is why half the amount is needed. These options are much less creamy and rich.

◀◀◀◀

"HONEY" MUSTARD DIPPING SAUCE

PREP: 5 minutes
CHILL: 4 to 6 hours or overnight
YIELDS: heaping ½ cup

. . . .

3 tablespoons (45g) Dijon
   mustard
3 tablespoons (45g) dairy-free
   plain yogurt
3 tablespoons (60g) coconut
   nectar
1 teaspoon (5g) fresh lemon juice
¼ teaspoon (1g) hot sauce
⅛ teaspoon ground turmeric

One of my favorite dipping sauces before becoming vegan was the honey mustard that's typically served with chicken fingers or fries. Well, friends, I have created a vegan version that's every bit as delicious! I use coconut nectar in place of the honey because it has a sweetness, thickness, and stickiness that is similar to honey. (Maple syrup just isn't going to cut it here.) Dairy-free yogurt acts as the "mayo"! If you'd like more heat, double the hot sauce.

Combine all the ingredients in a small bowl, and whisk until smooth. Place in the fridge to chill for 4 to 6 hours or overnight to intensify the flavors and slightly thicken. Store covered for 1 to 2 weeks in the fridge.

. . . .

Nutrition per about 2 tablespoons: 80 calories | 0.5g fat | 0.2g protein | 16.3g carbs | 0.3g fiber | 12.4g sugar | 290mg sodium

. . . .

NOTE When choosing a yogurt, make sure it is unflavored. I use coconut; however, Silk carries a soy yogurt that is plain but has a small amount of sugar in it. That will also work in this recipe since it is a sweet sauce. Do not use low-fat or almond yogurt.

SWEET CHILI-MUSTARD SAUCE

This has been the most popular simple sauce recipe on my blog for the past couple of years. This boldly flavored, virtually fat-free, all-purpose sauce takes 5 minutes to throw together but really stands out in a dish. (Be sure to use a whisk so it thickens well.) It tastes amazing on everything from burritos, tacos, and Mexican rice bowls to veggie burgers, salads, even as a dipping sauce for French fries. To tone down the heat, you can use 1½ tablespoons chili powder. I hope you enjoy finding many ways to use it.

Combine all the ingredients in a small bowl, and whisk really well until smooth. Taste and add more water as needed for desired taste and consistency.

. . . .

Nutrition per 2 tablespoons: 35 calories | 0.5g fat | 0.6g protein | 7.6g carbs | 0.6g fiber | 6.2g sugar | 167mg sodium

. . . .

NOTE Make sure you are using a standard American chili powder, which is a blend of different spices (see page 16 for more information about why that's important). If you cannot find one, then make my DIY blend on page 245.

PREP: 5 minutes
YIELDS: about 1 cup

. . . .

½ cup (120g) yellow mustard
¼ cup (80g) pure maple syrup
2 tablespoons (16g) mild chili powder or DIY Homemade Chili Powder (page 246)
2 to 4 tablespoons (30 to 60g) water

GREEN CHILE–LIME YOGURT SAUCE

PREP: 10 minutes
YIELDS: heaping 1 cup

. . . .

¼ cup (60g) cooked, peeled, and
    mashed Yukon Gold potato
1 (4.5-ounce) can green chiles,
    separated
1 tablespoon (15g) fresh lime juice
½ cup (120g) dairy-free plain
    yogurt
¼ teaspoon (1g) ground cumin
¼ teaspoon dried oregano
¼ teaspoon (2g) fine salt
⅛ teaspoon ground black pepper

Allow me to introduce you to the perfect sauce for inside or outside your burritos, nachos, or tacos. Heck, this stuff works over pretty much anything. I am guilty of sometimes eating it with a spoon. Oops! It is tangy and has a wonderful depth of flavor from the green chiles and lime juice. The potatoes give it a really smooth, thick, and creamy texture. My favorite way to serve this sauce is either over nachos or drizzled over my Cuban Black Bean–Stuffed Sweet Potatoes on page 134.

1. Add the potatoes, half of the green chiles, lime juice, yogurt, cumin, oregano, salt, and pepper to a food processor, and blend until completely smooth and no bits of potato remain.

2. Pour the sauce into a bowl, and stir in the remaining chiles. Taste and add more salt, if desired. Taste and add more lime juice, if more tartness is desired. Use immediately or place in the fridge to firm up for a few hours. The sauce will get thick in the fridge because it has potatoes in it, so just give it a good stir before using to make it perfectly smooth again.

. . . .

Nutrition per about 2 tablespoons: 36 calories | 0.7g fat | 1.3g protein | 6.1g carbs | 0.9g fiber | 0.4g sugar | 139mg sodium

. . . .

NOTE Cook your potato using your preferred method. To save time, I like to wrap mine well in plastic wrap, and cook it in the microwave on HIGH for 5 to 6 minutes or until really soft. Just peel the skin off and mash. For the yogurt, both soy and coconut work great.

MY FAVORITE BARBECUE SAUCE

This sauce was totally not planned to be in this chapter. I originally created it to go with my BBQ Chipotle Green Lentils on page 117, but I was so pleased with how it turned out that I had to include it by itself here. It embodies the flavor balance I like best in a barbecue sauce: perfectly tangy thanks to the dark balsamic, not too tomato-y (come on, it's not marinara), just enough sweetness, and some to-die-for smoky and spicy notes. Please do not sub with any other vinegar; it won't be the same!

Combine all of the ingredients in a small bowl, and whisk until completely smooth. Taste and add more chile pepper powder, if you'd like it spicier.

· · · · · · · · · · ·

Nutrition per 2 tablespoons: 21 calories | 0.1g fat | 0.7g protein | 4.9g carbs | 0.7g fiber | 3.4g sugar | 247mg sodium

· · · · · · · · · · ·

NOTE For a milder smoky heat, reduce the chipotle chile pepper powder to ¼ teaspoon (1g) or sub with Ancho chile powder, which has a very smoky flavor but is much less spicy than the chipotle. (I don't recommend omitting completely.) You could also use half and half of each.

PREP: 5 minutes
YIELDS: 1 cup + 2 tablespoons

· · · · · · · · · · · · · · · · ·

½ cup (120g) tomato paste
½ cup (120g) water
1 tablespoon (20g) pure maple syrup
1 tablespoon (15g) dark balsamic vinegar
1 teaspoon (3g) garlic powder
1 teaspoon (2g) smoked paprika
½ teaspoon (2g) ground chipotle chile pepper powder
½ teaspoon (3g) fine salt

ALL-PURPOSE LEMON CREAM

PREP: 5 minutes
YIELDS: 2 cups

. . . .

1 heaping cup (150g) raw, unsalted
    cashews
4 tablespoons (60g) fresh lemon
    juice
¾ cup (180g) water
1 teaspoon (4g) onion powder
¼ teaspoon (1g) ground black
    pepper
½ teaspoon (3g) fine salt

This is one of my go-to cream sauces to use on dishes where sour cream would traditionally be used as a condiment. While it is very creamy and tangy like sour cream, it is not supposed to replicate it. My favorite ways to use it are in burritos or tacos, as a topping for chili, or drizzled on potatoes.

Add all of the ingredients to a high-powered blender or food processor (see Note), and blend until completely smooth. Scrape the sides and blend again. You want it 100% smooth, like a heavy cream. Use immediately or place in the fridge to thicken. It will thicken a lot in the fridge overnight, so give it a good stir and let it come back to room temperature to loosen, if desired.

. . . .

Nutrition per 2 tablespoons: 55 calories | 4.4g fat | 1.5g protein | 3.3g carbs | 0.3g fiber | 0.6g sugar | 76mg sodium

. . . .

NOTE If you do not have a high-powered blender like a Vitamix, see the note on page 91 for substitutions. Alternatively, you can sub with raw cashew butter (see page 247 for how to make this) for the same amount, 150g, which is about 9 heaping tablespoons.

❧ *tip* ❧

For a nut-free version, sub the cashews with 1 cup (170g) cannellini beans if you don't mind bean-based sauces. Another option is to sub with ½ packed cup (120g) cooked, peeled, and mashed Yukon Gold potato. The potato thickens much more than cashews, which is why half the amount is needed. These options are much less creamy and rich.

❧

GARLIC–BLACK PEPPERCORN GRAVY

PREP: 10 minutes
COOK: 15 minutes
YIELDS: 1¾ cups

. . . .

½ cup (80g) finely diced yellow onion

3 extra-large garlic cloves (15g), minced

3 tablespoons (45g) water

4 tablespoons (40g) brown rice flour

1 cup (240g) low-sodium vegetable broth

1 teaspoon (4g) crushed black peppercorns or ½ teaspoon (2g) ground black pepper

1 teaspoon (1g) dried thyme

4 teaspoons (20g) gluten-free low-sodium soy sauce

1 cup (240g) creamy non-dairy milk

½ teaspoon (3g) fine salt

We all need a fabulous, foolproof gravy in our kitchen, and while I love the traditional brown-style gravy, I wanted to create something with a little bit more flair and excitement. Obviously, black pepper is a strong flavor here, so feel free to adjust (see the Note below). Make sure to dice the onion into tiny pieces so the gravy doesn't end up with large chunks. This pairs wonderfully with biscuits or The Best Fluffy "Buttermilk" Mashed Potatoes on page 176.

1. Add the onion, garlic, and 3 tablespoons water to a large stainless steel pan over medium heat. Bring to a low boil, and cook for about 8 minutes, stirring occasionally, until the onions are very tender.

2. Combine the flour and broth in a small bowl, and whisk until smooth. Add the flour mixture, black peppercorns, thyme, soy sauce, milk, and salt to the onion mixture, and whisk very well until smooth. Bring back to a boil, and then lower the heat to medium-low; cook for 5 to 10 minutes or until the gravy thickens to the desired consistency. (Keep in mind that it will thicken a bit as it cools.) Taste and add more salt, if desired.

. . . .

Nutrition per 2 tablespoons: 19 calories | 0.3g fat | 0.5g protein | 3.6g carbs | 0.4g fiber | 0.4g sugar | 154mg sodium

. . . .

NOTE If you're not gluten free, you can sub all-purpose flour for the brown rice flour, if you like. The peppercorns give this quite a peppery burst of flavor. If you are concerned this will be too peppery for you, then sub with ½ teaspoon (2g) ground black pepper, adding more at the end if you like. Or, if serving to kids, you may want to reduce to ¼ teaspoon (1g). For the non-dairy milk, cashew, soy, or "lite" coconut milk works wonderfully.

RESTAURANT-STYLE CHIPOTLE SALSA

PREP: 15 minutes
YIELDS: 3½ cups

. . . .

1 (28-ounce) can chopped
   tomatoes, undrained
½ cup (80g) diced red onion
2 tablespoons (30g) fresh lime
   juice
2 teaspoons (10g) minced garlic
¼ cup (32g) finely chopped fresh
   jalapeño (1 medium), stem and
   seeds removed
½ teaspoon (1g) ground cumin
½ teaspoon (1g) chipotle chile
   pepper spice
½ teaspoon (3g) fine salt
¼ to ½ cup (10 to 20g) loosely
   packed chopped fresh cilantro

Oh, how I love salsa. Chips and salsa were one of the things I always loved about Mexican restaurants growing up. It classifies as a meal, right? I like my salsa to be fairly smooth and not have big chunks of tomatoes. This version also has a good kick of chipotle spice to really amp up the flavor and smokiness with sweet red onion to balance out the acidity. Add the amount of cilantro that your cilantro-meter can handle. The salsa is good for about a week, if it lasts that long! I love to serve this alongside my Roasted Potato and Veggie Hash on page 48.

Add all of the ingredients to a food processor, and process about 30 seconds or until it all comes together into a semi-smooth texture with no big chunks of tomato. You may need to scrape the sides once and blend again. Serve immediately or place in the fridge for up to a week. It will thicken some as it sits in the fridge.

. . . .

Nutrition per ½ cup: 30 calories | 0.3g fat | 1.4g protein | 6.7g carbs | 1.8g fiber | 3.7g sugar | 174mg sodium

. . . .

CREAMY DIJON-PEPPER DRESSING

Nothing spruces up a salad quite like an incredible dressing. I love classics like Ranch and Caesar, but I'm not lying when I say this is my new favorite dressing. The punch of flavor from the Dijon mustard, the creaminess from the cashews, the kick of black pepper, and the depth from the sesame seeds makes this one amazing dressing. It is also great as a dip for veggies. If using the potato version, you will need to give it a good stir before using since it thickens a lot in the fridge. The bean version doesn't thicken as much.

1. Add all of the ingredients to a high-powered blender or food processor (see Note), and blend until completely smooth. Taste and add more salt, if desired. The dressing will be very runny at this point.

2. Place in the fridge for at least 2 hours or overnight. It will become much thicker.

. . . .

Nutrition per ¼ cup: 117 calories | 9.2g fat | 3.4g protein | 7g carbs | 1g fiber | 1.1g sugar | 240mg sodium

. . . .

NOTE If you do not have a high-powered blender like a Vitamix, see the note on page 91 for substitutions. Alternatively, you can sub with raw cashew butter (see page 247 for how to make this) for the same amount, 110g, which is about 7 tablespoons.

⇒ *tip* ⇐

For nut free, sub the cashews with the same amount of cannellini beans, but keep in mind, the results won't be as creamy or rich and it won't thicken up as well. To help with this, start with a couple of tablespoons less water, and then add more, if desired. Or, sub the cashews with 6 tablespoons (90g) tightly packed, cooked, peeled, mashed Yukon Gold potato. The potato thickens much more than cashews, which is why half the amount is needed.

PREP: 5 minutes

CHILL: 2 hours

YIELDS: 1½ cups

. . . .

¾ cup (110g) raw, unsalted cashews

¾ cup (180g) water

1½ teaspoons (9g) dark balsamic vinegar

1½ tablespoons (23g) fresh lemon juice

3 tablespoons (45g) Dijon mustard

1½ teaspoons (4g) toasted sesame seeds

½ teaspoon (2g) garlic powder

¾ teaspoon (2.5g) ground black pepper

⅜ teaspoon (2.25g) fine salt

EASY ENTRÉES

It is always my goal to create flavorful, filling, comforting food using easy and familiar ingredients. I don't aim to please just vegans or health enthusiasts, but everyone—meat-eaters and non-vegans included. Seriously, do you have to be vegan to love veggies, potatoes, or pasta? Nope!

   I also don't believe mealtime should require a million ingredients or steps. A short ingredient list doesn't mean you have to sacrifice flavor. With all of that in mind, I think you'll find this chapter delivers as promised. I have a few recipes that use chickpeas in different ways with completely different flavor combinations. I never realized how versatile and delicious they could be until I wrote this book!

SUMMERTIME SMOKY BBQ BOWL

PREP: 20 minutes
COOK: 35 minutes
YIELDS: 4 servings

. . . .

1½ cups (300g) dry white jasmine rice

1½ teaspoons (9g) fine salt, separated

2 large bell peppers, cut into strips (465g)

2 teaspoons (6g) DIY Homemade Chili Powder (page 245) or store-bought, separated

½ teaspoon (2g) ground black pepper, separated

2 (15-ounce) cans low-sodium pinto beans, drained and rinsed, or 3 cups cooked (510g)

1½ cups (200g) frozen sweet corn

1¼ cups (300g) Emergency Smoky Barbecue Sauce (page 226) or store-bought

1 large avocado (170g), sliced

¼ to ½ cup (25 to 50g) fresh sliced green onions

My favorite thing to eat growing up was barbecue—barbecue sauce is my favorite flavor. This bowl is inspired by those memories of my Dad cooking in the backyard during the hot Texas summers and us eating some grub. This bowl offers up beans, corn, bell peppers, avocado, and lots of barbecue sauce. You won't miss the meat, and you will be happily stuffed! Each serving is a large bowl, which could easily become five smaller bowls, if you'd prefer that. I like to use a mix of red, orange, and yellow bell peppers.

1. Add the rice, 2¼ cups (520g) water, and ½ teaspoon salt to a medium pot; bring to a boil. Once boiling, stir, cover, and turn down the heat to low. Simmer for 15 minutes or until all the water is gone. Remove from the heat (keep covered); let it steam for 5 minutes. Fluff with a fork and leave uncovered to cool for 5 minutes.

2. Meanwhile, add the bell peppers, 1 teaspoon chili powder, ½ teaspoon salt, ¼ teaspoon black pepper, and ½ cup (120g) water to a large pan over medium heat. Stir to coat the veggies well, cover, and cook for 5 to 8 minutes until the veggies are tender and the water has cooked away, stirring occasionally.

3. Meanwhile, add the beans to another pan or a microwave-safe bowl. Add ¼ cup (60g) water, remaining ½ teaspoon salt, remaining ¼ teaspoon black pepper, and remaining 1 teaspoon chili powder to the beans. Heat, covered, on the stove over medium heat for about 5 minutes or microwave for about 2 minutes. Heat the corn on the stove over medium heat for about 5 minutes or microwave for about 3 minutes.

4. Add the barbecue sauce to a small pot over medium-low heat, and cook for about 5 minutes or until very hot. If you're using my homemade BBQ sauce, you will want to cook it for 5 to 10 minutes to allow it to really bring out the flavors and thicken slightly.

5. Assemble the bowls by layering each with the rice, beans, corn, and bell peppers. Top with lots of barbecue sauce. Toss all of the ingredients together to coat everything with the barbecue sauce. Top with the avocado and green onions, and drizzle some extra barbecue sauce on top. If you want a more attractive presentation, you can showcase each ingredient by placing them side by side in a large bowl, and then drizzle with barbecue sauce.

. . . .

Nutrition per serving: 594 calories | 5.7g fat | 18.8g protein | 116g carbs | 18.5g fiber | 16.3g sugar | 1,423mg sodium

. . . .

NOTE Make sure you are using a standard American chili powder (see page 16 for more about why). If you cannot find one, make my DIY blend on page 245.

SOUTHWEST SWEET POTATO AND BLACK BEAN BOWL WITH CHIPOTLE CREAM

PREP: 25 minutes
COOK: 40 minutes
YIELDS: 6 servings

. . . .

1 cup (150g) raw, unsalted cashews

3 tablespoons fresh lime juice (45g)

1 to 2 tablespoons (20 to 40g) diced chipotles in adobo sauce

2 teaspoons (12g) fine salt, separated

1½ cups (270g) dry long-grain brown rice

2 large sweet potatoes, peeled and chopped into 1-inch chunks (about 7 cups [950g])

2 red bell peppers, cut into ½-inch strips (364g)

2 (15-ounce) cans low-sodium black beans, drained and rinsed, or 3 cups cooked (510g)

⅛ teaspoon ground black pepper

1½ cups (200g) frozen sweet corn

OPTIONAL: fresh chopped green onions, lime wedges

Tangy chipotle cream livens up this hearty bowl of sweet potatoes and beans. It makes it spicy and next level in flavor. Two tablespoons of chipotles give quite the kick, so reduce to one for a milder cream. For serving, add the cream to a ziplock bag, cut a tiny hole in one corner, and drizzle it all over the top.

1. Add the cashews, ½ cup (120g) water, lime juice, chipotles, and ¾ teaspoon salt to a high-powered blender or food processor (see Note); blend until completely smooth. Place the sauce in the fridge to thicken.

2. For fluffy rice, I recommend first rinsing it with cold water. Add the rice, 2¼ cups (540g) water, and ½ teaspoon salt to a medium pot and bring to a boil. Once boiling, reduce the heat to low, cover, and simmer for 25 to 30 minutes or until all the water is gone. Remove from the heat (keep covered), and let it steam for 10 minutes. Fluff with a fork and leave uncovered to cool for 5 minutes.

3. Preheat the oven to 415°F (213°C). Line 2 sheet pans with parchment paper.

4. Spread the potatoes in a single layer on one pan and the bell peppers on the other. Sprinkle ¼ teaspoon salt over the potatoes and a tiny pinch of salt (if desired) over the bell peppers. Roast the potatoes at 415°F for 15 minutes. Remove the pan from the oven, and toss the potatoes around. Place the pan with the potatoes on the top rack and the pan with the bell peppers on the bottom rack. Roast both for 15 minutes or until the potatoes are cooked through and golden brown and the bell peppers are tender and beginning to brown.

5. Meanwhile, add the beans to a bowl and season with the remaining ½ teaspoon salt and ⅛ teaspoon pepper. Add the corn to a separate bowl. Microwave the beans and the corn for a couple of minutes right before serving. Alternatively, if you prefer, heat them on the stove.

6. Assemble the bowls by layering each with rice, and then (layering remaining ingredients side by side) add the sweet potatoes, and then some beans next to the potatoes, then the corn, and then the bell peppers. Drizzle with the chipotle cream and, if desired, add extra lime juice, salt, pepper, and green onions.

. . . .

Nutrition per serving: 643 calories | 14.2g fat | 16.6g protein | 118g carbs | 15.4g fiber | 8.4g sugar | 1,010mg sodium

. . . .

NOTE If you do not have a high-powered blender like a Vitamix, see the note on page 91 for substitutions. Alternatively, you can sub with raw cashew butter (see page 247) for the same amount, 150g, which is about 9 heaping tablespoons.

❧ tip ❧

To make the chipotle cream nut free, sub the cashews with the same amount
of cannellini beans; but the results won't be as creamy or rich and it won't thicken up as well.
Start with just 6 tablespoons of water and add more, if desired. Or, sub the cashews with
½ packed cup (120g) cooked, peeled, mashed Yukon Gold potato. The potato thickens
much more than cashews, which is why half the amount is needed.

SWEET POTATO, CARAMELIZED ONION, AND RICE BUDDHA BOWL

PREP: 25 minutes
COOK: 45 minutes
YIELDS: 4 servings

. . . .

1½ cups (270g) dry long-grain brown rice

1¼ teaspoons (8g) fine salt, separated

2 large sweet potatoes, peeled and chopped into ¾-inch pieces (5 heaping cups [625g])

¼ teaspoon ground black pepper (1g), separated

1½ packed cups (240g) finely diced red onion

1 large poblano pepper, seeds removed and diced (75g)

1 large red bell pepper, diced (160g)

6 packed cups (162g) fresh spinach

1 (15-ounce) can low-sodium black beans, drained and rinsed, or 1½ cups cooked (255g)

4 tablespoons (60g) coconut aminos

OPTIONAL: toasted sesame seeds

I like to take familiar ingredients and give them completely different flavor profiles. The caramelized onions and coconut aminos add such a delicious sweetness to this bowl that really takes it up a notch. The sesame seeds are optional, but they do give a lovely crunch and nutty flavor to the bowls.

1. For fluffy rice, I recommend first rinsing it with cold water. Add the rice, 2¼ cups (540g) water, and ½ teaspoon salt to a medium pot; bring to a boil. Once boiling, stir, cover, and reduce to simmer for 25 to 30 minutes or until all the water is gone. Remove from the heat (keep covered), and let it steam for 10 minutes. Fluff with a fork and leave uncovered to cool for 5 minutes.

2. Meanwhile, preheat the oven to 425°F (220°C). Line a large sheet pan with parchment paper. Do not use foil, as the potatoes will stick.

3. Spread the chopped potatoes in a single layer on the prepared pan. Sprinkle ¼ teaspoon salt and ⅛ teaspoon pepper on the potatoes. Bake at 425°F for 20 minutes, flip, and cook 10 to 15 more minutes until tender and browned.

4. Meanwhile, add the onion, 3 tablespoons water, ¼ teaspoon salt, and ⅛ teaspoon black pepper to a large pan over medium heat. (A stainless steel pan works well to caramelize without any oil.) Stir well, and once the onions come to a simmer, stir-fry continuously until caramelized and nicely brown. Don't walk away, as they can burn. The water from the onions should keep them cooking as long as you keep stirring. This should take 5 to 8 minutes. They should have a nice brown color and be sweet and delicious. Transfer the onions to a small plate.

5. Add the poblano pepper, bell pepper, ¼ cup (60g) water, and ¼ teaspoon salt to the same pan you cooked the onions in. Turn the heat to medium-low, and cook until softened, stirring often, about 8 minutes. If needed, add just a touch of water to keep the veggies cooking. Transfer the peppers to a plate.

6. Add the spinach to the same pan with 2 tablespoons (30g) water and cook just a couple of minutes, stirring often, until wilted.

7. Heat the black beans in the microwave or on the stove.

8. To serve, place the rice at the bottom of a large serving bowl and top with the cooked onions, poblano and bell pepper mixture, sweet potatoes, spinach, and black beans. Drizzle with the coconut aminos, and toss everything to coat. I used about a tablespoon per bowl. Sprinkle the sesame seeds on top, if desired.

. . . .

Nutrition per serving: 516 calories | 2.7g fat | 14.3g protein | 110.6g carbs | 13.6g fiber | 16.7g sugar | 917mg sodium

. . . .

BBQ CHIPOTLE GREEN LENTILS WITH POTATO WEDGES

This dish has it all. It brings smoke and spice to the table in a big way. The BBQ sauce is straight-up drinkable. For the lentils, make sure they are fairly new and not too old, as that can affect them cooking properly. For the potatoes, I like to leave the skins on so they retain their shape better.

1. Rinse the lentils well. Add the lentils, 2¼ cups (540g) hot water, and ¼ teaspoon salt to a medium pot. Bring to a boil over high heat. Once boiling, cover, turn down the heat to low, and simmer for 30 to 35 minutes, or until the lentils are tender but still have a bite to them.

2. Meanwhile, preheat the oven to 400°F (200°C). Line a large sheet pan with parchment paper. Spread the potatoes on the pan in a single layer, being careful not to overlap them. Season with ¼ teaspoon salt and black pepper to taste. Bake at 400°F for 30 to 35 minutes or until golden brown. For extra crispiness, turn on your broiler, and broil for 1 to 2 minutes. Watch closely so they don't burn.

3. Meanwhile, add the tomato paste, ½ cup (120g) water, syrup, vinegar, garlic powder, paprika, chipotle chile pepper spice, and remaining ½ teaspoon salt to a bowl, and whisk until smooth. Set aside.

4. Once the lentils are tender, drain them well. Shake off any excess water. Add the lentils back to the pot, and stir in the BBQ sauce. Turn the heat down to medium and cook for a few minutes, stirring often, until the BBQ sauce thickens well and is no longer soupy. You want the lentils coated well in the thickened, but not runny, BBQ sauce. Once the potato wedges are done, serve with lentils on top and garnish with fresh green onions, if desired.

. . . .

Nutrition per serving: 370 calories | 1.1g fat | 21g protein | 72.1g carbs | 23.1g fiber | 11.2g sugar | 831mg sodium

. . . .

PREP: 20 minutes
COOK: 40 minutes
YIELDS: 3 servings

. . . .

1 cup (195g) dry green lentils

1 teaspoon (6g) fine salt, separated

2 pounds Yukon Gold potatoes (906g), cut into ½-inch wedges (about 6 cups)

½ cup (120g) tomato paste

1 tablespoon (20g) pure maple syrup

1 tablespoon (15g) dark balsamic vinegar

1 teaspoon (4g) garlic powder

1 teaspoon (2g) smoked paprika

¼ to ½ teaspoon (1 to 2g) chipotle chile pepper spice

OPTIONAL: ½ cup (55g) fresh sliced green onions

oil free • gluten free • nut free

PROTEIN-PACKED CURRY CHICKPEAS AND SWEET POTATO ROUNDS

PREP: 25 minutes
COOK: 40 minutes
YIELDS: 4 servings

. . . .

2 large sweet potatoes (1,000g), peeled and sliced into ¼-inch rounds

1¼ teaspoons (8g) fine salt, separated

1 large red bell pepper, diced (190g)

1 packed cup (160g) diced red onion

5 large garlic cloves (15g), minced

1½ tablespoons (18g) coconut sugar

4 teaspoons (9g) Curry Spice Blend (page 242) or store-bought yellow curry powder

½ teaspoon (1g) garam masala (optional)

¼ teaspoon (1g) ground black pepper

2 (15-ounce) cans low-sodium chickpeas, drained and rinsed, or 3 cups cooked (510g)

1 (13.5-ounce) can full-fat coconut milk

OPTIONAL: chopped fresh cilantro and limes for garnish

Chickpeas provide a nice dose of protein. They also take on the flavor profile of whatever you add to them, which makes them versatile. In this dish, the chickpeas soak up the bold mix of spices. Pairing them with sweet potatoes gives a unique twist instead of the usual rice and also balances out the spiciness beautifully. This dish gets its kick from a good dose of curry spice, so add a good squeeze of lime at the end to counteract it, if desired, as well as bring out the overall flavor. Be sure to use full-fat coconut milk. Anything else will be too watery. You could also serve this with cooked rice if you already have some on hand.

1. Preheat the oven to 425°F (220°C). Line a sheet pan with parchment paper.

2. Lay the sliced sweet potatoes in a single layer on the prepared pan and season with ¼ teaspoon salt and a pinch of black pepper. Bake at 425°F for 20 minutes on the first side, then flip them over, and bake 15 to 20 more minutes on the second side or until tender and starting to brown.

3. Meanwhile, add the bell pepper, onion, garlic, and ½ cup (120g) water to a large pan over medium heat. Bring to a simmer, and cook for 8 minutes, stirring occasionally, until the vegetables are tender. If needed, add just a tiny bit of water to keep them cooking. Add the coconut sugar; curry powder; remaining 1 teaspoon salt; garam masala, if desired; and black pepper to the pan; and cook, stirring, for about 30 seconds until fragrant and all the moisture is absorbed. Immediately add the chickpeas and coconut milk, and turn up the heat to medium. Bring to a simmer, cover, reduce the heat to medium-low, and cook for about 10 minutes or until the chickpeas are tender and the sauce has thickened some. You don't want to cook the sauce down too much. It should be just slightly thickened. If it thickens up too much, add a bit more milk and adjust the curry powder and spices, if needed. Taste and add more salt, if desired.

4. To serve, place the sweet potato rounds in a serving bowl and spoon the curry chickpeas alongside or on top of the potatoes. Garnish with fresh cilantro and a squeeze of lime juice, if desired.

. . . .

Nutrition per serving: 594 calories | 25.1g fat | 16.8g protein | 81.4g carbs | 17.4g fiber | 20.6g sugar | 1,127mg sodium

. . . .

SPICY AND SMOKY CHICKPEAS IN CREAMY TOMATO SAUCE

Spicy and smoky: Those two words just give me all the feels. They were the words that were the inspiration to liven up these chickpeas. This dish is anything but boring with a wonderful creamy tomato flavor. It is easily one of my favorite recipes ever. If you need less heat, reduce the chipotle chile pepper spice to ¼ teaspoon.

1. Add the rice, 1½ cups (360g) water, and ¼ teaspoon salt to a medium pot. Stir and bring to a boil. Once boiling, immediately cover and turn down the heat to low. Simmer for 15 minutes or until all the water is gone. Remove from the heat (keep covered), and let it steam for 5 minutes. Fluff with a fork and leave uncovered for 5 minutes to cool.

2. Meanwhile, add the onion and ½ cup (120g) water to a large saucepan over medium-low heat. Bring to a simmer, and cook for 5 minutes. Add the garlic, and cook for 3 more minutes, stirring often so the garlic doesn't burn.

3. Once the onions and garlic are tender, add the milk, tomato paste, smoked paprika, remaining 1 teaspoon salt, chipotle chile pepper spice, and chickpeas. Stir well, and bring to a simmer. Continue to cook for about 10 minutes until the chickpeas are soft and the liquid has thickened up to a nice sauce and is no longer watery. You want the sauce thickened, but not too thick. Serve immediately over the cooked rice.

. . . .

Nutrition per serving: 453 calories | 9.2g fat | 16.5g protein | 78.7g carbs | 12.4g fiber | 10.9g sugar | 1,059mg sodium

. . . .

NOTE For the milk, I use canned "lite" coconut milk, shaken well first. Another creamy milk like soy or cashew should work, too. I would not recommend light milks or the sauce will be watery.

PREP: 15 minutes
COOK: 20 minutes
YIELDS: 4 servings

. . . .

1 cup (200g) dry white jasmine rice

1¼ teaspoons (8g) fine salt, separated

¾ packed cup (120g) finely diced red onion

4 large garlic cloves, minced (12g)

1¼ cups (300g) "lite" canned coconut milk, shaken well

¼ cup + 2 tablespoons (90g) tomato paste

2 teaspoons (6g) smoked paprika

½ teaspoon (2g) chipotle chile pepper spice

2 (15-ounce) cans low-sodium chickpeas, drained and rinsed, or 3 cups cooked chickpeas (510g)

OPTIONAL: 3 tablespoons (12g) fresh chopped parsley for garnish

TIME-SAVER CAJUN RED BEANS AND RICE

PREP: 20 minutes
COOK: 20 minutes
YIELDS: 4 servings

. . . .

2 teaspoons (4g) Cajun Spice Seasoning (page 241) or store-bought

½ tablespoon (4g) smoked paprika

2 tablespoons (20g) brown rice flour

2 teaspoons (12g) fine salt, separated

¼ teaspoon (1g) ground black pepper

1½ cups (300g) dry white jasmine rice

1 packed cup (160g) diced red onion

1 large green bell pepper, diced (160g)

5 extra-large garlic cloves, minced (18g)

2 (15-ounce) cans low-sodium red beans or kidney beans, drained and rinsed, or 3 cups cooked (510g)

OPTIONAL: 1 teaspoon (5g) dark balsamic vinegar; chopped fresh green onions and chopped fresh thyme for garnish

Without a doubt, one of my all-time favorite meals to eat growing up and before I switched to a vegan diet was red beans and rice. I have the original version on my blog, but since this book is all about comforting foods in an easier and quicker way, I came up with this much faster version. This one is just as delicious but ready so fast! Before beginning the rice, have all your veggies chopped and ready so that everything will be warm at the same time. If you need less heat, decrease the Cajun spice to 1½ teaspoons. The balsamic vinegar adds another depth of flavor, but it's not crucial to the recipe.

1. Add the Cajun seasoning, paprika, flour, 1½ teaspoons salt, and black pepper to a small bowl, and whisk well. Set aside.

2. Add the rice, 2¼ cups (540g) water, and the remaining ½ teaspoon salt to a medium pot and stir. Bring to a boil, cover, immediately turn down the heat to low, and simmer for 15 minutes until all the water is gone. Remove from the heat (keep covered), and let it steam for 5 minutes. Fluff with a fork and leave uncovered for 15 minutes to cool.

3. Meanwhile, add the onion, bell pepper, garlic, and ½ cup (120g) water to a large pot or large, deep saucepan over medium-high heat. Cook for about 5 minutes, stirring often, or until the veggies are beginning to get tender. Most of the water should be gone. Add the reserved mixed seasoning mixture to the veggies, and stir constantly for about 1 minute or until it soaks up the moisture.

4. Add 1½ cups (360g) water and the beans, and stir well. Bring to a simmer, cover, turn down the heat to low, and cook for 10 to 15 minutes or until the beans and veggies have reached the desired tenderness and the mixture has thickened a bit but is still saucy so you really get the flavor of the broth over the rice. My sweet spot was right at 12 minutes. Taste and add more salt or Cajun Spice Seasoning, if desired. If using the balsamic vinegar, add it now to the beans.

5. Ladle the red beans into bowls and scoop out the rice to place on top. Garnish with fresh green onions and thyme, if desired.

. . . .

Nutrition per serving: 439 calories | 0.4g fat | 13.9g protein | 92.9g carbs | 11.6g fiber | 6.3g sugar | 1,289mg sodium

. . . .

NOTE You can use a store-bought Cajun seasoning if desired, but make sure it is a no-salt version. If gluten isn't a concern, you can sub all-purpose flour for the brown rice flour.

SKILLET BAKED MAC 'N' CHEESE

Kid-approved, husband-approved, non-vegan approved. Even though it's just 8 ingredients (plus salt, black pepper, and water), this recipe has depth and rich flavor. Be sure to use a neutral-flavored milk here—avoid almond or rice milks, as they will ruin the taste and texture. For the Dijon, use half for a milder taste or sub with ½ to 1 tablespoon white vinegar. If you want a kick of heat, add some red pepper flakes at serving.

1. Add 8 cups (1,920g) water to a large pot, and bring to a boil. Add the pasta and ½ tablespoon salt to the water, and stir well. Cook for about 8 minutes or until al dente, stirring a couple of times while it cooks.

2. Preheat the oven to 350°F (176°C).

3. Add the cashews, 1 cup plus 2 tablespoons yogurt (270g), soy milk, Dijon mustard, 2¼ teaspoons paprika, garlic powder, 1¾ teaspoons salt, and ¼ teaspoon black pepper to a high-powered blender or food processor (see Note), and blend for 1 to 2 minutes or until completely smooth. Scrape the sides once during blending. You want it 100% smooth.

4. Once the pasta is al dente, drain it well, but do not rinse. Add it back to the pot, and pour the cheese mixture over it. Stir gently until the pasta is coated well; add to a 10-inch cast-iron skillet or an 8-inch square glass or ceramic baking dish.

5. Add the panko, the remaining ½ teaspoon paprika, the remaining ½ teaspoon salt, and a pinch of black pepper to a bowl, and stir well. Add the remaining 2 tablespoons yogurt, and press the mixture together with the back of a spoon or fork until all the crumbs are moistened and loose. Sprinkle them evenly over the pasta. Loosely place a piece of foil over the pasta but do not tighten it around the edges. This step is important so the pasta doesn't dry out while baking.

6. Bake at 350°F for 10 minutes, then remove the foil, and preheat oven to high broil. Broil for 3 to 5 minutes or until the top gets toasty brown. Do not walk away, as it can quickly burn! Serve immediately.

· · · · · · · · · · ·

Nutrition per serving: 381 calories | 12.5g fat | 11.1g protein | 60.1g carbs | 4.1g fiber | 7.9g sugar | 1,042mg sodium

· · · · · · · · · · ·

NOTE If you do not have a high-powered blender like a Vitamix, see the note on page 91 for substitutions. Or, sub with raw oil-free cashew butter (114g), which is about 7 tablespoons. For the yogurt, I use So Delicious "unsweetened coconut," which has no sugar. The Silk brand "soy plain" has a small amount of sugar, but it still works without any detectable sweetness. I would advise against almond or low-fat varieties.

PREP: 15 minutes
COOK: 30 minutes
YIELDS: 6 servings

· · · · · · · · · · · · · · · · ·

12 ounces (340g) elbow or
   fusilli pasta
3¾ teaspoons (23g) fine salt,
   separated
¾ cup (114g) raw, unsalted
   cashews
1¼ cups (300g) plain
   unsweetened dairy-free soy
   or coconut yogurt, separated
1 cup (240g) creamy plain soy milk
1 tablespoon (15g) Dijon mustard
2¾ teaspoons (7g) paprika,
   separated
½ teaspoon (2g) garlic powder
¼ teaspoon (1g) ground black pepper
¾ cup (60g) plain oil-free panko
   (Japanese-style breadcrumbs)

OPTIONAL: red pepper flakes

➳ *tip* ➺

To make this gluten free, sub the wheat pasta with a spiral-variety brown rice pasta, as it holds its shape best. For the breadcrumbs, sub with gluten-free panko.

⟪⟪⟪⟪⟪⟪

CHEESY MEXICAN TORTILLA BAKE

PREP: 20 minutes
COOK: 20 minutes
YIELDS: 9 squares

. . . .

1 cup (150g) raw, unsalted
cashews

2 cups (480g) smooth salsa,
separated

¾ cup (180g) plain unsweetened
dairy-free yogurt

1¼ teaspoons (3g) smoked paprika

1¼ teaspoons (3g) ground cumin

¾ to 1 teaspoon (5 to 6g)
fine salt

9 (6-inch) corn tortillas, cut into
fourths (36 pieces total)

2 (15-ounce) cans low-sodium
black beans, drained, rinsed,
and patted dry, or 3 cups
cooked (510g), separated

2 cups (293g) frozen sweet corn,
separated

OPTIONAL: sliced fresh
green onions, hot sauce

➤ tip ⬉

To make this nut free, sub the
cashews with the same amount of
white beans, making sure to blend
well. Please note that this is only
recommended if you cannot have
cashews or are closely watching
your fat intake, as the dish does
taste bean-y and is less creamy.

⬅⬅⬅⬅⬅

This recipe from my blog became so popular with every type of eater out
there that I had to put it in this book. Picky kids, teenagers, and meat-loving
husbands all love it. For the salsa, use a mild heat for the kiddos and medium
for the adults.

1. Preheat the oven to 375°F (190°C).

2. Add the cashews, 5 tablespoons (75g) water, 1 cup salsa (240g), yogurt,
paprika, cumin, and ¾ teaspoon salt to a high-powered blender or food
processor (see Note), and blend until completely smooth and no bits remain.
Taste and add the extra ¼ teaspoon salt, if desired.

3. Pour one-third of the cheese sauce on the bottom of an 8-inch square baking
dish, spreading out evenly with a spoon. Place 6 tortilla pieces in a row on top
of the sauce. Repeat the process with 12 more tortilla pieces, creating 3 rows
(18 tortilla pieces total for the bottom layer). Add 1 can of the beans on top of
the tortilla pieces, spreading out evenly. Add the remaining 1 cup salsa on top
of the beans, spreading out evenly. Spread 1 cup of the corn on top of the salsa.
Layer another one-third of the cheese sauce on top of the corn, spreading out
evenly and making sure to reserve plenty for the top layer.

4. Repeat the steps by adding the remaining tortilla pieces in rows, then the
beans and corn. Spread the remaining cheese sauce evenly over the corn with
the back of a spoon, covering the top well. Loosely place a piece of foil on top
of the dish. This is so the cheese sauce doesn't bake up and harden too quickly.

5. Bake at 375° for 15 minutes, remove the foil, and bake for 5 to 10 more
minutes or until the cheese sauce has a nice, firm, orange-brown look on the
edges only. If you prefer the cheese to be more firm, just bake it a bit longer.
Keep in mind that the longer you bake it, the drier the top cheese layer becomes
after it is removed from the oven. Garnish with green onions and a dash of hot
sauce, if desired.

. . . .

Nutrition per square: 287 calories | 9.9g fat | 9.6g protein | 43.1g carbs | 8g fiber |
8g sugar | 568mg sodium

. . . .

NOTE If you do not have a high-powered blender like a Vitamix, see the note
on page 91 for substitutions. Alternatively, you can sub with raw cashew butter
(see page 247 for how to make this) for the same amount, 165g, which is about
10 tablespoons. For the yogurt, I recommend soy or coconut yogurt for this,
not almond or low-fat. While yogurt will yield the best results in both taste and
texture, if you cannot find it, sub with vegan sour cream.

LEMON-BASIL CREAM SAUCE WITH VESUVIO PASTA AND TOMATOES

Think you need oil to make a creamy basil sauce? Using a creamy low-fat coconut milk and pumpkin seeds is my secret to this amazing nut-free basil sauce. Garnish with extra fresh basil leaves, if you like, and serve with fresh bread.

1. Preheat the oven to 375°F (190°C). Line a sheet pan with parchment paper.

2. Cut the tomatoes in half and spread them out evenly on the pan. Lightly season with salt and pepper, if desired. Bake at 375°F for 15 to 20 minutes or until the tomatoes are bursting, tender, and juicy.

3. Meanwhile, add 16 cups (3,840g) water to a large pot, and bring to a boil. Add the pasta and 1 tablespoon salt to the water, and stir well. Cook for 10 to 13 minutes or until al dente. Drain the pasta well, but do not rinse. Add it back to the pot.

4. Meanwhile, add the basil, coconut milk, garlic, lemon juice, pumpkin seeds, remaining ½ teaspoon salt, and black pepper to a blender or food processor, and blend until completely smooth. Taste and add more salt or lemon juice, if desired. This makes 2 cups sauce.

5. Divide the pasta and sauce evenly among bowls. Top with the tomatoes and red pepper flakes.

. . . .

Nutrition per serving: 474 calories | 13.9g fat | 20.4g protein | 70g carbs | 10.6g fiber | 2.6g sugar | 374mg sodium

. . . .

NOTE You can sub with any spiral pasta you like, or a gluten-free variety, if needed. I used "lite" coconut milk for this because it's really creamy and helps make the oil-free sauce rich. If allergic to coconut, you can sub with cashew or soy, but keep in mind it will be less creamy and change the flavor.

PREP: 10 minutes
COOK: 15 minutes
YIELDS: 6 servings

. . . .

¾ cup (155g) cherry tomatoes

6 cups (520g) wheat Vesuvio pasta

3½ teaspoons (21g) fine salt, separated

4 packed cups (80g) fresh basil leaves

1 cup (240g) canned "lite" coconut milk, shaken first

4 small garlic cloves (10g)

3 to 4 tablespoons (45 to 60g) fresh lemon juice

¾ cup (132g) raw, unsalted pumpkin seeds (pepitas)

½ teaspoon (2g) ground black pepper

1 teaspoon (2g) red pepper flakes

NEXT-LEVEL RED SAUCE WITH TAGLIATELLE PASTA

PREP: 15 minutes
COOK: 30 minutes
YIELDS: 6 servings

. . . .

1 packed cup (160g) diced red onion
½ packed cup (80g) diced red
    bell pepper
5 extra-large garlic cloves,
    minced (18g)
¼ cup (60g) dry red wine, such
    as Cabernet Sauvignon or Merlot
2 (14.5-ounce) cans diced fire-
    roasted tomatoes, undrained
1 tablespoon (4g) Italian seasoning
1 tablespoon (18g) + ¼ teaspoon
    (2g) fine salt, separated
¼ teaspoon (1g) ground black pepper
¼ packed cup (8g) fresh basil
    leaves
¼ teaspoon red pepper flakes
    (optional)
16 ounces (500g) tagliatelle pasta

OPTIONAL: chopped fresh basil,
    red pepper flakes for garnish

❧ tip ❧

If you avoid red wine, simply
sub with broth instead. I would
suggest also adding a tablespoon
of dark balsamic vinegar with
the broth for an extra punch
of flavor. It produces a similar
flavor to a rich wine.

One of the best at-home meals is one that makes a gourmet presentation but takes just minutes to prepare. This is one of those. It is not your everyday spaghetti-style sauce but is truly *next level*. It's an I-belong-in-a-restaurant type of sauce. This recipe comes together quickly, so have all of your veggies and ingredients prepared and ready to go before beginning. Make sure you don't rinse the pasta since rinsing washes away the starch on the surface, which is what helps the sauce stick. Fresh bread goes great with this!

1. Add the onion, bell pepper, garlic, and ½ cup (120g) water to a large pan over medium heat. Cook for 8 minutes until the veggies are softened, stirring occasionally. Add the wine, and cook for about a minute, stirring the whole time. Add the tomatoes, Italian seasoning, ¼ teaspoon salt, and black pepper, and bring to a low boil. Cover, reduce the heat to low, and simmer for 15 minutes to let the flavors develop and slightly thicken. Add the basil and, if desired, the red pepper flakes, and cook for just about 30 seconds or until the basil is just wilted.

2. Meanwhile, add about 16 cups (3,840g) water to a large pot, and bring to a boil. Once boiling, add the pasta and the remaining 1 tablespoon (18g) salt, and stir quickly. Cook for 5 to 6 minutes or until al dente. Drain the pasta, but do not rinse.

3. Add the sauce to a blender, and blend until smooth. If you like a chunky sauce, just partially blend it. I like a really smooth sauce, so I completely puree it. Taste and add more salt, black pepper, or red pepper flakes, if desired. This yields 4 cups of sauce.

4. To serve, divide the pasta among bowls and top with the sauce. Garnish with fresh basil and more red pepper flakes, if desired.

. . . .

Nutrition per serving: 333 calories | 1.2g fat | 11.6g protein | 67.2g carbs | 4.5g fiber | 7.9g sugar | 526mg sodium

. . . .

NOTE If you cannot find Italian seasoning, then sub with 1 teaspoon (1g) dried oregano, ¾ teaspoon dried thyme, ¾ teaspoon dried basil, and ½ teaspoon dried rosemary. You can use your pasta of choice. If a gluten-free sub is needed, I like brown rice spiral.

❧ oil free • gluten free • nut free ❧

MY FAVORITE SAVORY MEATLESS BEAN BALLS

Packed with flavor and spice, these meatless bean balls are my absolute top choice to serve with spaghetti and sauce—a total comfort meal—or in sub sandwiches. The Worcestershire and tomato paste are crucial, adding a wonderful depth and savory flavor. Use 1 teaspoon of chili powder if you'd prefer milder meatless balls. Make sure to follow each step closely, as this will ensure the texture turns out correctly—nice and crispy on the outside but moist and soft on the inside.

1. Add the onion and 3 tablespoons (45g) water to a small stainless steel pan over medium heat. Bring to a simmer, and cook for 5 minutes, stirring occasionally. Once the water is gone, cook for 3 more minutes, stirring constantly, to brown the onions a bit. This will give the balls a lot of flavor. Turn the heat down if the onion is browning too quickly.

2. Preheat the oven to 375°F (190°C). Line a sheet pan with parchment paper.

3. Add the cooked onions, chickpeas, tomato paste, and Worcestershire to a food processor, and pulse several times or just until the chickpeas are broken up into smaller pieces and have a rough, chunky texture. Don't puree this. You will need to scrape the sides after the first pulse. If there are whole chickpeas remaining, then mash them with a fork so no whole chickpeas remain. Set aside.

4. Add the chili powder, paprika, salt, pepper, cornmeal, and rice flour to a large bowl, and whisk well. Add the chickpea mixture to the spice mixture; stir and press the mixture together for several minutes until it is well moistened and comes together. Using your hands, form the mixture into a sticky, cohesive ball. You will need to rotate and knead the mixture several times.

5. Scoop 1½ tablespoons of chickpea mixture out, and press together to form a ball. The mixture is too delicate to roll into balls with my palms, but I found placing a ball in one hand while pressing and piecing it together with my fingertips worked well. Just make sure each ball is compact and smooth. This will yield 15 balls. Place them on the prepared pan.

6. Bake at 375°F for 15 minutes, flip over, and bake 15 more minutes. Let cool for 10 to 15 minutes so they can firm up. Store any extra in the fridge.

7. If desired, serve with pasta and sauce. Add the desired amount of sauce to a large stainless steel pan over medium-low heat. Add only the balls you want to eat at that time to the sauce and rotate them carefully for 3 to 4 minutes or until heated through. The balls will soften too much if stored in the sauce overnight.

· · · · · · · · · · ·

Nutrition per serving: 158 calories | 2.3g fat | 6.3g protein | 29.8g carbs | 5.8g fiber | 5.4g sugar | 519mg sodium

· · · · · · · · · · ·

PREP: 25 minutes
COOK: 38 minutes
YIELDS: 5 servings

· · · · · · · · · · · · · · · · ·

¾ packed cup (120g) finely diced red onion

1 (15-ounce) can low-sodium chickpeas, drained, rinsed, and patted dry, or 1½ cups cooked (255g)

4 tablespoons (60g) tomato paste

2 tablespoons (30g) vegan Worcestershire

1 to 2 teaspoons (2 to 5g) mild chili powder

1 teaspoon (3g) smoked paprika

½ teaspoon (3g) fine salt

¼ teaspoon (1g) ground black pepper

¼ cup (40g) fine cornmeal

¼ cup (40g) brown rice flour

OPTIONAL: hot cooked pasta, chopped fresh parsley, Easiest-Ever Pizza/Spaghetti Sauce (page 230) for serving

CUBAN BLACK BEAN–STUFFED SWEET POTATOES

PREP: 20 minutes
COOK: 45 minutes
YIELDS: 6 servings

. . . .

6 large sweet potatoes (3,000g)
1 large red bell pepper, diced (160g)
½ cup (80g) finely diced red onion
4 large garlic cloves, minced (12g),
    or 2 teaspoons (8g) garlic
    powder
½ tablespoon (2g) dried oregano
1 teaspoon (3g) ground cumin
1 teaspoon (6g) fine salt
¼ teaspoon (1g) ground black
    pepper
2 (15-ounce) cans low-sodium
    black beans, drained and rinsed,
    or 3 cups cooked (510g)
1 (4-ounce) can mild green chiles

OPTIONAL: Green Chile–Lime
Yogurt Sauce (page 96),
chopped fresh cilantro for
serving

These classic black beans are a very simple Cuban dish that taste incredible stuffed inside a perfectly baked sweet potato. It's a simple meal but delicious and healthy. I recommend sprinkling with cilantro and drizzling with my tangy Green Chile–Lime Yogurt Sauce—it is divine! For a simpler topping, top each with sliced avocado and fresh lime juice.

1. If you're making the Green Chile–Lime Yogurt Sauce, then prepare that now and keep it stored in the fridge until serving time. It is so, so delicious on this!

2. Preheat the oven to 400°F (200°C). Place the sweet potatoes on a pan lined with parchment paper. Bake at 400°F for 45 minutes to 1 hour or until the potatoes are tender but not mushy. This will vary depending on their size.

3. When there is about 15 minutes left of baking time for the potatoes, start the beans. Add ¼ cup (60g) water, bell pepper, onion, and garlic cloves (if using the powder, add it in Step 4) to a large pan over medium heat. Cook about 8 minutes, stirring occasionally, until the veggies are tender. If needed, add just a tiny bit of water to keep them cooking.

4. Stir in another ½ cup (120g) water, garlic powder (if using in place of fresh), oregano, cumin, salt, black pepper, and the beans. Reduce the heat to medium-low, and cook just a few minutes to heat through and cook away water. Stir in half or more of the can of green chiles depending on how spicy you want it. Taste and add more salt or pepper, if desired.

5. Spoon the beans over each baked potato and top with lots of the Green Chile–Lime Yogurt Sauce, if desired.

. . . .

Nutrition per serving: 536 calories | 0.6g fat | 17.6g protein | 116.5g carbs | 26.2g fiber | 29.7g sugar | 908mg sodium

. . . .

TERIYAKI PATTIES

These are my best-loved patties to date and make the most delicious burgers. They are flavored with teriyaki sauce, sweet caramelized onions, toasted sesame seeds, and garlic. They are so hearty and chewy, and they don't fall apart. Be sure to use quick-cooking oats (not old-fashioned)—they are crucial to the texture and binding. For a spicier burger patty, add in the red pepper flakes. If not, increase the black pepper to ¾ teaspoon.

1. Preheat the oven to 350°F (177°C). Line a sheet pan with parchment paper.

2. Add the rice, 1 cup (240g) water, and ¼ teaspoon salt to a medium pot and stir. Bring to a boil, cover, reduce the heat to low, and simmer for 30 to 35 minutes or until all the water is gone. Remove from the heat (keep covered), and let it steam for 5 minutes. Fluff with a fork and leave uncovered for 15 minutes to cool.

3. Meanwhile, add the onion and 3 tablespoons (45g) water to a pan over medium-low heat. Bring to a simmer, cook 5 minutes, stirring occasionally, until the onions are tender. Once the water is gone, stir the onions constantly for a couple of minutes to brown them. Add the onions to a food processor, along with the teriyaki sauce, sesame seeds, garlic powder, black pepper, and, if desired, red pepper flakes. Pulse to combine the spices with the sauce and break up the onions a bit, but not puree them. Add the chickpeas and pulse several times to break up the chickpeas into tiny pieces, but do not puree them. Add the cooled rice, rice flour, and oats, and pulse several times until it all comes together into sticky chunks. You want the mixture to hold together but do not want to overmix it.

4. Transfer the mixture to a bowl. Use a ½-cup measuring cup to scoop out the chickpea mixture, pressing it into the cup to flatten it. Plop the patty out into your hand, shape into a ball, and place on the prepared pan. Press down until the chickpea mixture is 1 inch thick, and shape the edges into a round patty. Repeat the procedure with the remaining chickpea mixture to get 6 patties total.

5. Bake at 350°F for 20 minutes, flip them over, and bake 10 more minutes. Let cool for 10 to 15 minutes. The patties firm up on the insides a lot as they cool.

6. To serve, I like to dress buns with lots of teriyaki sauce, lettuce, and extra sesame seeds, but choose whatever toppings you prefer. Store leftover patties in the fridge wrapped tightly in plastic wrap and placed in an airtight container. These reheat well in the microwave and also in the oven on low heat.

. . . .

Nutrition per patty: 191 calories | 3.8g fat | 6.5g protein | 33.3g carbs | 3.8g fiber | 3.8g sugar | 513mg sodium

. . . .

PREP: 25 minutes
COOK: 40 minutes
YIELDS: 6 large patties

. . . .

½ cup (90g) dry brown jasmine or long-grain rice

¼ teaspoon (2g) fine salt

½ packed cup (80g) finely diced red onion

½ cup (120g) Sesame Teriyaki Sauce (page 229) or store-bought

3 tablespoons (27g) toasted sesame seeds

2 teaspoons (8g) garlic powder

½ teaspoon (2g) ground black pepper

¼ to ½ teaspoon (0.5 to 1g) red pepper flakes (optional)

1 (15-ounce) can low-sodium chickpeas, drained and rinsed, or 1½ cups cooked (255g)

6 tablespoons (60g) brown rice flour

¾ cup (75g) gluten-free quick-cooking oats

OPTIONAL: buns, lettuce, tomato slices, and any burger toppings desired, for serving

tip

If you make my homemade teriyaki sauce, make it the day before or early in the day so that it is chilled and thickened. If you don't have chickpeas on hand, white beans of any kind will work.

ULTIMATE BBQ BEAN BALL SUB

PREP: 25 minutes
COOK: 38 minutes
YIELDS: 4 sandwiches

. . . .

½ cup (100g) dry white jasmine rice

⅛ + ¾ teaspoon (5g) fine salt, separated

½ packed cup (80g) finely diced red onion

1 (15-ounce) can low-sodium chickpeas, drained and rinsed, or 1½ cups cooked (255g)

1¾ cups (420g) Emergency Smoky Barbecue Sauce (page 226) or store-bought, separated

1½ teaspoons (6g) garlic powder

2 teaspoons (6g) DIY Homemade Chili Powder (page 245) or store-bought

¼ teaspoon (1g) ground black pepper

¾ cup (84g) gluten-free quick-cooking oats

4 (3.1-ounce) pieces sub sandwich bread

⇀ *tip* ↽

I strongly recommend my homemade barbecue sauce (uncooked) for this recipe, as it literally takes 5 minutes to whip up and is to die for. Use your favorite gluten-free bread, if needed, and note that nutrition can vary greatly depending on the bread you use.

Did I mention that I love barbecue flavors? These BBQ-inspired bean balls are chewy and hearty thanks to chickpeas, rice, and oats. While they are not meant to resemble actual meat, they certainly do take on a similar hearty texture. Be sure to use quick-cooking oats, not regular old-fashioned oats, and white jasmine rice for the right texture and so that the balls bind well.

1. Add the rice, ¾ cup (180g) water, and ⅛ teaspoon salt to a small pot and stir. Bring to a boil, cover, immediately turn down the heat to low, and simmer for 15 minutes or until all the water is gone. Remove from the heat (keep covered); let it steam for 5 minutes. Fluff with a fork and leave uncovered for 15 minutes to cool.

2. Meanwhile, add the onion and 3 tablespoons (45g) water to a small pan over medium-low heat. Cook for about 8 minutes or until the onions are tender. Once the water evaporates, stir continuously until they caramelize a bit, 1 to 2 minutes, and then remove from the heat.

3. Preheat the oven to 375°F (190°C). Line a sheet pan with parchment paper.

4. Add the cooked onion and chickpeas to a food processor; pulse about 10 times until all the chickpeas are broken up and no longer whole. You want it to have a rough, crumbly texture. Set aside.

5. Add ¾ cup (180g) barbecue sauce, garlic powder, chili powder, the remaining ¾ teaspoon salt, and pepper to a large bowl, and whisk well. Add the crumbly chickpeas, oats, and cooled rice. Using a fork, press and stir the mixture around for several minutes until it all comes together in a sticky batter. It will seem crumbly at first, but keep stirring and pressing the mixture together and it will come together.

6. Once the mixture is thick and sticking together, form the balls using about 2 tablespoons worth of the mixture for each. Press the mixture with your hands and roll into compact balls. Don't rush this step. Place the balls on the prepared pan. Every 3 balls or so, wipe the palms of your hands with a paper towel. Repeat until you get 16 balls total.

7. Bake at 375°F for 15 minutes, flip them over, and bake 10 more minutes. If you want yours to be extra chewy, bake them for 14 to 15 minutes on the second side. Let the balls cool for 10 to 15 minutes as they will firm up a lot while they cool.

8. Add the remaining 1 cup (240g) barbecue sauce and the balls to a large pan. Heat over medium-low, gently tossing the balls in the sauce to coat them well and warm everything through, about 5 minutes. Place the bean balls in your sub sandwich bread with any extra sauce, and chow down!

. . . .

Nutrition per sandwich: 450 calories | 3.5g fat | 14.9g protein | 90.5g carbs | 6.2g fiber | 18g sugar | 1,634mg sodium

COMFORTING SOUPS & STEWS

Soup, how I love thee. I could eat soup every day of my life, regardless of the weather—it's my favorite food, hands down. I also love stews and chilis. To me, there is no better definition of comfort food than a warm bowl of something flavorful and satisfying that's perfectly balanced in taste and texture.

This chapter features an appetizing collection of recipes that are easy to make, tasty, and brimming with wholesome and super-filling ingredients. Whether you are craving creamy and comforting or light and healthy, I've got you covered. I hope this chapter becomes just as much a favorite of yours as it is mine.

ULTIMATE BROCCOLI-CHEESE SOUP

PREP: 20 minutes
COOK: 30 minutes
YIELDS: 4 servings

. . . .

5 heaping cups (300g) broccoli florets

1 ¾ teaspoons (10g) fine salt, separated

¼ + ⅛ teaspoon (1.5g) ground black pepper, separated

2 heaping cups peeled ¼-inch pieces Yukon Gold potatoes (300g)

1 packed cup (160g) finely chopped yellow onion

¾ cup (114g) raw, unsalted cashews

¾ cup (180g) tomato sauce

½ cup (120g) unsweetened plain coconut yogurt

2 teaspoons (10g) apple cider vinegar

1 ¼ teaspoons (3g) smoked paprika

OPTIONAL: ⅛ teaspoon cayenne pepper, 2 tablespoons (12g) nutritional yeast, cubed bread, sliced fresh green onions

This soup is comfort food in a bowl. It is creamy, rich, and every bit as amazing as the dairy version I grew up eating.

1. Preheat the oven to 375°F (190°C). Line a sheet pan with parchment paper.

2. Spread the broccoli out on the prepared pan, and season with ¼ teaspoon salt and ⅛ teaspoon pepper. Bake at 375°F for 15 to 20 minutes or until tender and beginning to brown on top but still firm.

3. Meanwhile, add the potatoes, 3 cups (720g) water, onion, and ½ teaspoon salt to a pot over medium heat. Bring to a simmer, and cook until the potatoes are tender, about 10 minutes.

4. Meanwhile, add the cashews, tomato sauce, yogurt, vinegar, paprika, remaining 1 teaspoon salt, remaining ¼ teaspoon pepper, and, if desired, cayenne and nutritional yeast to a high-powered blender or food processor (see Note), and blend until completely smooth. Scrape the sides as needed. Set aside.

5. Once the cooked potatoes are tender, immediately remove the pan from the heat. Add the potato mixture, including the water, to the blender. Blend until completely smooth. Be careful not to overblend or the starch in the potatoes will release too much and make the texture too glue-like. You only need to blend until just combined. Taste and add more salt or spices, if desired.

6. Pour in bowls and top with the roasted broccoli. Garnish with cubed bread and fresh green onions, if desired.

. . . .

Nutrition per serving: 339 calories | 15.1g fat | 10.4g protein | 47.4g carbs | 7.5g fiber | 9.5g sugar | 1,301mg sodium

. . . .

NOTE If you do not have a high-powered blender like a Vitamix, you'll need to soak your cashews for 8 hours or preferably overnight in a bowl of warm water to soften, and then drain, rinse, and proceed with the recipe. Otherwise, the soup will be gritty. If using soaked cashews, a food processor works better than a regular, non-high-powered blender. Alternatively, you can sub with raw cashew butter (see page 247 for how to make this) for the same amount, 114g, which is about 7 tablespoons. If using store-bought, make sure to use a raw cashew butter with no added oil.

ITALIAN SWEET POTATO AND CARROT SOUP

I absolutely LOVE this soup. It is beautifully simple, creamy, and comforting. The natural sweetness from the sweet potatoes and carrots gives it a lovely flavor while the optional toasted pepitas add a nice crunch to the creamy texture (although the soup is still great without them). If you want a spicy kick, add a pinch of cayenne. Making the pepitas is super easy. Add the pepitas to a small pan over medium-low heat, and stir constantly while they get toasty brown, 2 to 3 minutes. They will pop, so don't lean over the pan too closely. And do not walk away, as they can quickly go from toasty to burnt.

1. Add the onion, garlic, carrots, and ¾ cup of the broth to a large pot over medium heat. Bring to a simmer, and cook about 8 minutes or until the carrots are just tender, stirring occasionally. Add the remaining 2¼ cups broth, Italian seasoning, salt, and pepper, and stir well. Stir in the sweet potatoes, and bring back to a boil over high heat. Once boiling, reduce the heat to medium-low, and cook about 15 minutes or until the sweet potatoes are fork tender. Stir in the milk and 1 tablespoon lemon juice, and remove from the heat.

2. Transfer to a blender or puree with a hand blender. Be careful, as the mixture will be really hot. Blend just until smooth and the potatoes and carrots are no longer whole, or until the desired texture is achieved. Taste and add more salt or up to 1 tablespoon lemon juice, if desired. Garnish with toasted pepitas, if desired.

. . . .

Nutrition per serving: 168 calories | 1g fat | 4.1g protein | 36g carbs | 5.4g fiber | 9g sugar | 1,677mg sodium

. . . .

PREP: 20 minutes
COOK: 25 minutes
YIELDS: 4 servings

. . . .

½ packed cup (80g) diced yellow onion

3 large garlic cloves, minced (10g)

3 medium carrots (127g), sliced into ¼-inch-thick rounds

3 cups (720g) low-sodium vegetable broth, separated

1 tablespoon (4g) Italian seasoning

2 teaspoons (12g) fine salt

¼ teaspoon (1g) ground black pepper

4 heaping cups (520g) peeled and chopped sweet potatoes, cut into ½-inch pieces

¾ cup (180g) creamy soy or plant-based milk

1 to 2 tablespoons (15 to 30g) fresh lemon juice, separated

OPTIONAL: ½ cup (80g) raw, unsalted pumpkin seeds (pepitas), toasted

tip

For the Italian seasoning, make sure it is one without any added salt or red pepper flakes. If you cannot find this, sub with ½ tablespoon (1g) dried oregano, ½ teaspoon dried thyme, ½ teaspoon dried basil, and ½ teaspoon dried rosemary.

HEARTY ITALIAN WHITE BEAN–BASIL SOUP

PREP: 10 minutes
COOK: 17 minutes
YIELDS: 6 servings

. . . .

4½ cups (1,080g) low-sodium vegetable broth

½ cup (104g) dry white jasmine rice

1¼ cups (300g) tomato sauce, separated

1 packed cup (160g) finely chopped yellow onion

4 large garlic cloves, minced (16g)

1 tablespoon + 1 teaspoon (4g) Italian seasoning

1½ teaspoons (9g) fine salt

¼ teaspoon (1g) ground black pepper

½ teaspoon (1g) red pepper flakes (optional)

2 (15-ounce) cans low-sodium white beans, drained and rinsed, or 3 cups cooked (510g)

½ cup (24g) finely chopped fresh basil

OPTIONAL: fresh basil

Here it is! This is a tastier and easier version of one of the most popular soup recipes on my blog. I make this soup more than any other because it is delicious and so incredibly fast to make! Adding a bit of the tomato sauce at the end helps to brighten the soup.

1. Add the broth, rice, 1 cup of the tomato sauce, onion, garlic, Italian seasoning, salt, black pepper, and, if desired, red pepper flakes to a large pot over high heat, and stir well. Bring to a boil, reduce the heat to medium-low, cover with the lid tilted to allow some steam to escape, and cook for 10 minutes to really infuse the broth with flavor and to allow the onions and rice to become tender. Stir a couple of times to make sure the rice isn't sticking to the bottom.

2. Once the rice is tender, add the beans. If the rice isn't tender, cook another minute or so until it is before adding the beans. Bring to a simmer over medium-low heat, and cook for about 5 minutes, stirring occasionally. Add the fresh basil and the remaining ¼ cup tomato sauce. Heat the basil through for a couple of minutes, and then remove the soup from the heat. Keep in mind that the soup will seem quite thin at first but will thicken up from the rice as it sits over the next 10 minutes or so. The soup will thicken up more overnight like a thick stew because of the rice. Taste and add more salt or tomato sauce, if desired. Serve with more fresh basil and red pepper flakes, if desired.

. . . .

Nutrition per serving: 202 calories | 1.5g fat | 8.7g protein | 39g carbs | 6.8g fiber | 3g sugar | 1,266mg sodium

. . . .

> *tip*

For the dried Italian seasoning, make sure it is one without any added salt or red pepper flakes. If you cannot find this, sub with 2 teaspoons dried oregano, ¾ teaspoon dried thyme, ¾ teaspoon dried basil, and ½ teaspoon dried rosemary.

BBQ SWEET POTATO AND BEAN SOUP

I like my soups and stews to have a strong flavor so that it feels like nothing is missing. My all-time favorite flavor is anything with barbecue sauce. Sweet potatoes complement and further enhance the sweet notes of the barbecue sauce in this recipe. You can use any combination of beans for this soup. I usually use a mix of pinto and black beans.

1. If using my homemade barbecue sauce, make it first. It only takes 5 minutes! Note that for this soup, you will not be heating the sauce up, as directed in that recipe. Just use it immediately after making it.

2. Add the onion, bell pepper, garlic, and ½ cup of the vegetable broth to a large pot over medium heat. Once it begins to bubble, cook for 8 minutes or until the onion and bell pepper are beginning to get tender and the broth is about gone. Add the remaining 2½ cups broth, chili powder, salt, black pepper, sweet potatoes, and barbecue sauce. Stir well, and increase the heat to high. Once it begins to boil all over, cover, and reduce the heat to medium-low; cook for 10 minutes or until the sweet potatoes are tender but not mushy. This time may vary depending on the size of your potatoes. Add the beans, and heat through for about 5 minutes. Taste and add more spices, if desired. Serve with sliced green onions, if desired.

. . . .

Nutrition per serving: 253 calories | 0.5g fat | 10.1g protein | 52.7g carbs | 12.9g fiber | 12g sugar | 893mg sodium

. . . .

PREP: 25 minutes
COOK: 25 minutes
YIELDS: 6 servings

. . . .

1 cup (240g) Emergency Smoky Barbecue Sauce (page 226) or store-bought

1 packed cup (160g) finely chopped yellow onion

1 large green bell pepper, diced (180g)

4 large garlic cloves, minced (16g)

3 cups (720g) low-sodium vegetable broth, separated

1 tablespoon (8g) mild chili powder

1 teaspoon (6g) fine salt

¼ teaspoon (1g) ground black pepper

4 rounded cups (520g) peeled and chopped sweet potatoes, about ½-inch-thick pieces

2 (15-ounce) cans low-sodium preferred beans, drained and rinsed, or 3 cups cooked (510g)

OPTIONAL: ½ cup (55g) fresh sliced green onions

❧ tip ❧

Make sure you are using a standard American chili powder (see page 16 for more information about why this is important). If you cannot find one, then make my DIY blend on page 245.

GREEN SPLIT PEA SOUP WITH CORIANDER

PREP: 15 minutes
COOK: 70 minutes
YIELDS: 4 servings

. . . .

1 packed cup (160g) diced yellow onion

4 large garlic cloves, minced (12g)

3 large carrots, sliced into ¼-inch rounds (236g)

6 cups (1,440g) low-sodium vegetable broth, separated

1½ cups (315g) dry, unsoaked green split peas

2 teaspoons (10g) liquid smoke

1 teaspoon (2g) ground coriander

1 teaspoon (6g) fine salt

½ teaspoon (2g) ground black pepper

2 tablespoons (30g) fresh lemon juice

OPTIONAL: cayenne pepper or hot sauce for serving

Who doesn't love a classic green split pea soup? Of course, traditionally it's made with ham and the veggies are cooked in oil. Well, I can promise you that this soup is rightfully scrumptious without either of those. I added a surprising ingredient, coriander, and it gives incredible flavor to this twist on the classic. For a stronger smoky flavor, reserve ½ teaspoon of the liquid smoke to stir in at the very end just before serving. Make sure you are using peas that are not old, as that can prevent them from softening properly. Look them over to make sure there is no debris in the batch, then rinse well with warm water and set aside. Dried legumes can vary greatly in their cooking time, so check them at 40 minutes to see if they are soft enough and continue cooking until they reach your desired tenderness. Mine took around an hour, but yours may take longer.

1. Add the onion, garlic, carrots, and ¾ cup of the broth to a large pot over medium heat. Bring to a simmer, and cook about 8 minutes, stirring occasionally, until the carrots are almost fully tender. Add the remaining 5¼ cups broth, peas, liquid smoke (reserving ½ teaspoon for adding at the end for a stronger smoky flavor, if desired), coriander, salt, and pepper, and stir well. Turn the heat to high, and bring to a boil. Once boiling, cover, reduce the heat to low, and simmer for 45 minutes to an hour or until the peas are completely tender, thickened, and slightly mushy. You are going to need to stir the soup a few times during the cooking to ensure the peas cook evenly. They will break up on their own and thicken the soup beautifully.

2. Add the lemon juice and reserved ½ teaspoon liquid smoke at this time (if you choose this option). Taste and add more salt, if desired. Ladle the soup into bowls, and serve with a pinch of cayenne or hot sauce, if desired.

. . . .

Nutrition per serving: 338 calories | 1g fat | 20.5g protein | 61.4g carbs | 22.6g fiber | 12.6g sugar | 1,431mg sodium

. . . .

HUNGARIAN RED LENTIL SOUP

Dinner doesn't have to take forever. This recipe comes together fast, thanks to red lentils and easy ingredients. The Hungarian paprika, dry mustard, and tomato paste give this simple dish a wonderful depth of flavor. This soup goes great with some fresh crusty bread!

PREP: 15 minutes
COOK: 23 minutes
YIELDS: 5 servings

. . . .

1. Add the onion, carrots, garlic, and 1 cup (240g) water to a medium pot over medium heat. Bring to a simmer, and cook for 8 minutes, stirring a couple of times during, or until the veggies are tender but not overly so. Remove the pan from the heat, and add the lentils, 2½ cups (600g) water, tomato paste, paprika, dry mustard, salt, and pepper. Stir well, and bring to a boil over high heat. Cover, reduce the heat to low, and simmer for 10 minutes.

2. Add the milk, and increase the heat to medium-low; cook 5 to 10 minutes or until the lentils are tender yet still firm, and the soup thickens some. Stir often, and do not overcook, as you don't want the lentils to become mushy. Taste and add more salt, if desired. Serve immediately.

. . . .

Nutrition per serving: 223 calories | 4.6g fat | 12g protein | 37.3g carbs | 7.9g fiber | 5.9g sugar | 878mg sodium

. . . .

NOTE Make sure the paprika you are using is not hot paprika. For the milk, it is important to use a creamy milk like cashew or "lite" coconut milk here for best results. The "lite" coconut milk is very creamy but yields no coconut taste. Almond and rice milks don't do well, and definitely don't use full-fat coconut, as it is too rich and thick and will ruin the flavor.

1 packed cup (160g) diced yellow onion

3 medium carrots (154g), cut into ¼-inch-thick slices

3 large garlic cloves, minced (15g)

1 cup (209g) dry red lentils, rinsed well with cold water

6 tablespoons (90g) tomato paste

2 tablespoons (15g) Hungarian sweet paprika

1 teaspoon (2g) dry mustard

1½ teaspoons (9g) fine salt

¼ teaspoon (1g) ground black pepper

1 cup (240g) canned "lite" coconut milk, well shaken

THAI RICE NOODLE AND BOK CHOY SOUP

PREP: 15 minutes
COOK: 10 minutes
YIELDS: 4 servings

. . . .

1 tablespoon (15g) minced garlic

1-inch knob (10g) fresh ginger, minced

2 (13.6-ounce) cans or 3 cups (720g) "lite" coconut milk

3½ tablespoons (52g) gluten-free low-sodium soy sauce

¼ cup (60g) red Thai curry paste

2 to 3 tablespoons (24 to 36g) coconut sugar

3 heads baby bok choy, leaves only (75g)

3.5 ounces (100g) skinny vermicelli rice noodles

OPTIONAL: toasted sesame seeds, sliced fresh green onions, red pepper flakes for garnish

I love it when a super-simple and quick recipe turns out to be absolutely delicious. This soup is one of those. It is aromatic, loaded with lots of fresh ginger and garlic flavors, and has a wonderful creamy element from the coconut milk. I'm slightly embarrassed to admit how fast I ate this. Using ¼ cup of the Thai paste makes it fairly spicy. You can reduce the amount to 3 tablespoons, but you may need to add extra soy sauce at the end.

1. Add the garlic, ginger, 2 cups (480g) water, coconut milk, soy sauce, curry paste, and coconut sugar to a medium pot, and whisk until smooth. Bring to a boil, reduce the heat to medium, and cook for 5 minutes to infuse the coconut milk mixture with flavor.

2. Meanwhile, remove the stalks from the bok choy, and discard. (They are too fibrous, and you don't want them in the soup.) Cut the bok choy leaves into strips. The sliced leaves should equal about 4 lightly filled cups (75g). Add the bok choy strips to the soup, and cook for 3 minutes or until they are beginning to get tender.

3. Add the rice noodles, and stir to incorporate the noodles into the soup. Remove from the heat, and let sit for about 5 minutes for the noodles to soak up the coconut milk mixture and tenderize. As they sit, the noodles will thicken up the soup beautifully. Taste and add more soy sauce, if desired. Garnish with sesame seeds, green onions, red pepper flakes, and a few extra fresh bok choy leaves, if desired.

. . . .

Nutrition per serving: 249 calories | 10g fat | 5.1g protein | 38.5g carbs | 4.1g fiber | 7.6g sugar | 769mg sodium

. . . .

⇒ *tip* ⇐

It's important to use the super-skinny rice noodles for this soup, as they soak up the liquid really well. The package may or may not say vermicelli on it and may just say rice noodles or rice sticks. You can find them in the Asian food section of most grocery stores. Other traditional noodles will not work in this soup.

ITALIAN HERB–ROASTED RED PEPPER BISQUE

The combo of roasted red bell peppers and sweet potatoes is out of this world. I'm a big lover of roasted red bell peppers for their deep flavor. The addition of dried herbs and chili powder really packs a ton of flavor. The soup is creamy, lowfat, and filling.

1. Preheat the oven to 400°F (200°C).

2. Line a sheet pan with foil. Place the bell peppers on the foil, and roast at 400°F for 25 minutes or until well charred. Set aside to cool a bit before handling.

3. Add the onion and ½ cup (120g) water to a large sauté pan over medium heat. Cook for about 5 minutes or until the onions are translucent. Add the garlic, and cook 2 minutes. Remove from the heat.

4. Once the peppers have cooled a bit to handle, remove and discard the stems and seeds. Add the peppers to a blender, using as much of the pepper juice as possible and all of the charred, blackened skins because that is where all the flavor is! Add the cooked onion and garlic, coconut milk, sweet potato, lemon juice, Italian seasoning, chili powder, and salt to the blender, and blend until completely smooth and no skins remain. Taste and add more salt and pepper, if desired. Pour into bowls and garnish with fresh basil and an extra squeeze of lemon juice, if desired.

· · · · · · · · · · ·

Nutrition per serving: 177 calories | 5.5g fat | 3.7g protein | 30.1g carbs | 6g fiber | 13.5g sugar | 633mg sodium

· · · · · · · · · · ·

NOTE Regarding the "lite" coconut milk, it is necessary for the creaminess and richness of the soup. Light milks like almond, rice, or oat will not do well here. You can cook the sweet potato in the microwave on HIGH for 6 to 8 minutes or until very soft, and then peel and mash. Or, roast the sweet potato (whole) at the same time as the peppers for 45 minutes or so until completely soft. For the Italian seasoning, make sure it is one without any added salt or red pepper flakes. If you cannot find this, sub with 1 tablespoon (2g) dried oregano, 1 teaspoon dried thyme, 1 teaspoon dried basil, and ½ teaspoon dried rosemary.

PREP: 15 minutes
COOK: 38 minutes
YIELDS: 5 servings

· · · · · · · · · · · · · · · · ·

4 red bell peppers (708g)

1 packed cup (160g) diced red onion

4 large garlic cloves, minced (15g), or 2 teaspoons (8g) garlic powder

1 (13.6-ounce) can or 1½ cups (360g) "lite" coconut milk

1 packed cup (248g) cooked, mashed sweet potato

2 tablespoons (30g) fresh lemon juice

1½ tablespoons (6g) Italian seasoning

4 teaspoons (11g) mild chili powder

1¼ teaspoons (9g) fine salt

OPTIONAL: fresh sliced basil, fresh lemon juice

❧ *tip* ❧

Make sure you are using a standard American chili powder (see page 16 for more about why). If you cannot find one, then make my DIY blend on page 245.

CAJUN VEGGIE AND POTATO CHOWDER

PREP: 25 minutes
COOK: 30 minutes
YIELDS: 6 servings

. . . .

½ cup (75g) raw, unsalted
   cashews

1 packed cup (160g) finely diced
   yellow onion

1½ tablespoons (5g) fresh thyme
   leaves or 1 tablespoon (2g) dried

2 teaspoons (5g) Cajun Spice
   Seasoning (page 241)

3 tablespoons (45g) Dijon
   mustard

¼ teaspoon (1g) ground black
   pepper

1¼ teaspoons (6g) fine salt

4 cups (590g) peeled, chopped
   Yukon Gold potatoes (about
   ½-inch pieces)

4 medium carrots, cut into
   ¼-inch pieces (120g)

1 cup (136g) frozen sweet corn

OPTIONAL: fresh thyme leaves
   and sprigs for garnish

This chowder came about because of my husband's love of the Cajun food he grew up eating in Louisiana. My love for all things creamy and my obsession with potatoes joined together with Cajun spices and veggies for what turned out to be the most comforting chowder I've ever eaten. You'll need to have all your veggies chopped and ready before beginning since the soup cooks fairly fast. Use 1½ teaspoons Cajun Spice Seasoning if you'd like less heat.

1. Add the cashews and 1 cup (240g) water to a high-powered blender or food processor (see Note). Blend until completely smooth and creamy. This is your cashew cream.

2. Add the onion and ½ cup (120g) water to a medium pot over medium heat. Bring to a simmer, and cook about 8 minutes, stirring often, or until the onion is tender and the water is gone.

3. Add 2 cups (480g) water, the thyme, Cajun Spice Seasoning, mustard, pepper, and salt, and stir well. Stir in the potatoes and carrots. (The mixture will be rather chunky and it won't seem like there's enough liquid, but there will be plenty to cook it while covered.) Bring to a boil, cover, and reduce the heat to medium-low. Cook for 8 to 10 minutes or until the potatoes are just tender but still firm.

4. Add the cashew cream and corn, and cook on medium-low for 5 to 10 minutes or until the mixture starts to thicken, stirring often. Taste and add more salt or spices, if desired. Garnish with additional fresh thyme, if desired. Serve immediately.

. . . .

Nutrition per serving: 193 calories | 6.6g fat | 5.2g protein | 31.7g carbs | 5.5g fiber | 5.3g sugar | 592mg sodium

. . . .

NOTE The key to this chowder is the homemade cashew cream. Do not use store-bought cashew milk or any other milks—it does not work! Trust me on this; it will be watery and gross. If you do not have a high-powered blender like a Vitamix, see the note on page 142 for substitutions. If you are nut free, sub with 1 cup (240g) "lite" canned coconut milk, shaken well. Do not use full-fat, as it is too thick and will make the soup taste like coconut. This is the only milk sub that works!

SWEET POTATO–LENTIL COMFORT STEW

Stew and the word comfort just go together, don't they? I love stews because, if done right, they should have nice big chunks of veggies that are beautifully coated with a well-flavored broth. This stew has protein-packed lentils, carb-rich sweet potatoes, and a dreamy red wine broth.

PREP: 15 minutes
COOK: 40 minutes
YIELDS: 5 servings

. . . .

1. Add the onion, garlic, and ¾ cup of the broth to a large pot over medium heat. Bring to a simmer, and cook for 5 minutes or until softened. Add the wine, and cook for 3 to 5 minutes. Add the remaining 4 cups broth and the lentils, bring to a high boil, reduce the heat to low, and simmer for 10 minutes. This is to kick-start the softening process for the lentils before adding the tomato sauce, which can slow down the cooking of the lentils.

2. Add the sweet potatoes, tomato sauce, Italian seasoning, salt, and pepper, and stir well. Bring to a high boil, cover, reduce the heat to low, and simmer for 15 to 20 minutes or until the lentils and sweet potatoes are tender but not mushy. Lentils can vary greatly on how fast or slow they cook, so they may take longer than 20 minutes.

. . . .

Nutrition per serving: 284 calories | 0.3g fat | 14.7g protein | 53g carbs | 10.4g fiber | 11.7g sugar | 1,337mg sodium

. . . .

NOTE For the Italian seasoning, make sure it is one without any added salt or red pepper flakes. If you cannot find this, sub with 1 tablespoon (2g) dried oregano, 1 teaspoon dried thyme, 1 teaspoon dried basil, and 1 teaspoon dried rosemary.

1½ cups packed (240g) diced white onion

1½ tablespoons (23g) minced garlic

4¾ cups (1,140g) low-sodium vegetable broth, separated

¾ cup (180g) Cabernet Sauvignon or Merlot

1½ cups (300g) dry green lentils

3 heaping cups (393g) peeled, chopped sweet potatoes (about 1-inch chunks)

1 cup (240g) tomato sauce

2 tablespoons (7g) Italian seasoning

2 teaspoons (12g) fine salt

1 teaspoon (3g) ground black pepper

SMOKY WHITE BEAN AND POTATO STEW

PREP: 25 minutes
COOK: 45 minutes
YIELDS: 6 servings

. . . .

7 heaping cups (1,120g) peeled, chopped Yukon Gold potatoes (about ½-inch pieces), separated

2 ¾ teaspoons (16g) fine salt, separated

½ + ⅛ teaspoon (2.5g) ground black pepper, separated

2 poblano peppers (250g), cut into ¼-inch strips

1 packed cup (160g) diced white onion

6 cups (1,440g) low-sodium vegetable broth, separated

1 tablespoon (15g) minced garlic

2 teaspoons (4g) smoked paprika

¼ teaspoon (1g) chipotle chile pepper spice (optional)

1 teaspoon (5g) liquid smoke (optional)

4 (15-ounce) cans low-sodium cannellini white beans, drained and rinsed, or 6 cups cooked (1,020g)

3 tablespoons (45g) vegan Worcestershire

OPTIONAL: red pepper flakes for garnish

This stew has it all. It has an incredibly thick and hearty texture and is smoky, filling, protein-packed, and full of flavor. This is a blog recipe that's gotten a makeover: It's quicker and more flavorful. Make sure to toss the seeds out when slicing the poblano peppers or they will be really hot!

1. Divide the chopped potatoes into 5 cups and 2 cups. The 5 cups will be cooked into the soup and the other 2 will be roasted as garnish.

2. Preheat the oven to 400°F (204°C). Line a sheet pan with parchment paper.

3. Add 2 cups (320g) of the chopped potatoes to the pan; sprinkle with ¼ teaspoon salt and ⅛ teaspoon black pepper. Roast at 400°F for 10 minutes. Add the poblano peppers and a pinch of salt to the pan, and cook for 10 minutes or until the potatoes and peppers are tender. Preheat the broiler, and broil for 2 minutes, watching them closely, or just until they turn golden brown.

4. Meanwhile, add the onion and ¼ cup of the broth to a large pot over medium heat, and bring to a simmer. Cook for 5 minutes, add the garlic, and cook 2 more minutes, stirring often to keep from burning. Add the remaining 5 ¾ cups broth, paprika, remaining 2 ½ teaspoons salt and ½ teaspoon black pepper, and, if desired, the chipotle chile pepper and liquid smoke. Stir well. Add the remaining 5 cups (800g) of the potatoes, increase the heat to high, and bring to a boil. Once boiling, reduce the heat to medium, cover, and cook for 15 to 20 minutes or until the potatoes are tender but not too soft. Add the beans and Worcestershire, and stir well. Cook for 10 more minutes or until the beans are soft.

5. Turn off the heat, and using a potato masher or a stick blender, mash about half of the soup (or as much as you like), and then give it a good stir to combine. Top with the roasted potatoes, poblano peppers, and, if desired, red pepper flakes.

. . . .

Nutrition per serving: 443 calories | 0.6g fat | 17.9g protein | 93g carbs | 18.6g fiber | 8g sugar | 1,484mg sodium

. . . .

SECRET INGREDIENT THREE-BEAN CHILI

I love chili. I'm from Texas and grew up eating tons of it, and this one is my favorite. It includes salsa, smoked paprika, and a very surprising ingredient— sweet potatoes! Not only do the sweet potatoes thicken it up and make the chili more hearty, the flavor is amazing with the heat. You can use a mix of beans, such as 1 can black beans, 1 can pinto beans, and 1 can white beans, for a range of color. You can cook and mash the sweet potato while the onions are cooking.

1. Add the onion and bell pepper and ¼ cup (60g) water to a medium pot over medium heat. Bring to a simmer, and sauté the vegetables for about 5 minutes, stirring occasionally, until the onions are soft and the water has basically cooked off.

2. Add 2 cups (480g) water, the salsa, chili powder, cumin, salt, paprika, black pepper, cayenne pepper, if desired, and beans. Stir really well, increase the heat, and bring to a boil. Once boiling, cover, reduce the heat to low, and simmer for 20 minutes or until the beans have softened some and the chili has thickened a little. Don't worry if it's not too thick, as the potato will thicken it a lot. Taste and add more chili powder, cayenne, or salt, if desired.

3. Stir in the mashed sweet potato. Remove from the heat, and serve immediately. It should be nice and thick with some liquid still remaining. Garnish with red onion and avocado, and serve it with Sweet Potato Cornbread.

. . . .

Nutrition per serving: 262 calories | 2.8g fat | 12.9g protein | 48.5g carbs | 13.9g fiber | 9.6g sugar | 1,054mg sodium

. . . .

NOTE Regarding the salsa you use, make sure it is a flavor you love, as it will be reflected in the chili, including the heat level. I used a chipotle salsa that has a medium heat level and it tasted amazing in this. If you are worried about it being too spicy, use a mild salsa.

PREP: 20 minutes
COOK: 30 minutes
YIELDS: 6 servings

. . . .

1 packed cup (160g) finely diced red onion

1 large diced red bell pepper (160g)

½ cup (120g) smooth salsa

3 tablespoons (24g) mild chili powder

½ tablespoon (4g) ground cumin

1½ teaspoons (9g) fine salt

1¼ teaspoons (3g) smoked paprika

¼ teaspoon (1g) ground black pepper

¼ teaspoon (1g) cayenne pepper (optional)

3 (15-ounce) cans low-sodium chili beans or 4½ cups cooked (765g)

½ cup cooked, peeled, mashed sweet potato (120g)

OPTIONAL: diced red onion, sliced avocado for garnish; Sweet Potato Cornbread (page 179) for serving

❧ tip ❧

Make sure you are using a standard American chili powder (see page 16 for more about why this is important). If you cannot find one, then make my DIY blend on page 245.

≪≪≪≪←

❧ 8 ❧

SIDES & DIPS

Sides and dips are often an afterthought, but they can be just as much fun as the main dish. This chapter will prove that. These sides can liven up an entrée or are so good that you might just make them the meal by grouping them together. And if there is one thing I like to make (and eat), it is dips of all varieties. Anything flavorful that you can stick a chip or cracker in is a win in my book. And they can totally be dinner. If it's healthy and full of wholesome ingredients, then why not?

I think you'll find these recipes are anything but ordinary, and they were created particularly to be hits with guests. No ho-hum hummus or side salads here, friends.

ALMOND-COATED ASPARAGUS WITH DIJON-TAHINI SAUCE

PREP: 10 minutes
COOK: 8 minutes
YIELDS: 4 to 6 servings

. . . .

½ cup (67g) almond meal

½ teaspoon (3g) fine salt, separated

½ teaspoon (2g) ground black pepper, separated

8 ounces (227g) fresh asparagus, ends cut off (about 2 inches)

½ of a lemon

¼ cup (64g) toasted tahini

2 tablespoons (30g) Dijon mustard

2 tablespoons (30g) soy or cashew milk

2 tablespoons (30g) fresh lemon juice

4 teaspoons (22g) pure maple syrup

This side dish goes well with mashed potatoes and lentil loaves. The almond meal combined with lemon creates a Parmesan cheese-like flavor, which was a total accident but a welcome surprise. The Dijon-Tahini Sauce also doubles as a delicious salad dressing.

1. Preheat the oven to 425°F (220°C). Line a sheet pan with parchment paper.

2. Add the almond meal, ¼ teaspoon salt, and ¼ teaspoon pepper to a large bowl, and whisk to combine.

3. Place the asparagus on a large platter or plate, and squeeze the lemon juice evenly all over. Place the asparagus, a few at a time, in the almond meal mixture, and rotate to coat them with the mixture. Lay them flat on the prepared pan. Repeat with the remaining asparagus, making sure not to overlap on the pan.

4. Bake at 425°F for 8 to 9 minutes or until tender but still firm. Depending on how thick your asparagus is, you may need to bake them a couple extra minutes. Check one with a fork before removing the whole pan from the oven.

5. To make the sauce, add the tahini, mustard, milk, lemon juice, syrup, remaining ¼ teaspoon salt, and remaining ¼ teaspoon pepper to a small bowl, and whisk until smooth. Taste and season with salt or pepper, if desired. Drizzle the sauce over the asparagus and serve immediately. The sauce will thicken in the fridge. Store it in the fridge up to 1 week.

. . . .

Nutrition per serving (based on 4): 207 calories | 15.1g fat | 6.6g protein | 12.8g carbs | 3.5g fiber | 5.1g sugar | 486mg sodium

. . . .

≽ *tip* ≼

To make this nut free, sub the almond meal with finely ground raw, unsalted sunflower kernels. It will change the flavor a little.

≺≺≺≺≺

SKILLET MEXICAN CORN

I really love this side dish: the smells, the flavor, the kick of heat from the fresh jalapeño. Mmmm, so good! The super-sweet corn is perfectly balanced with the heat and warm spices and punch of fresh lime juice. If you need less heat, use ½ jalapeño. This goes great as a side to tacos, burritos, or even Mexican veggie/bean burgers.

1. Heat ½ cup (120g) water in a large skillet or cast-iron skillet over medium-high heat. Once the water comes to a simmer, add the onion, bell pepper, jalapeño, ½ teaspoon of the salt, and black pepper, and stir well. Cook for about 8 minutes, stirring often, until the veggies are tender and the water is gone.

2. Meanwhile, prepare the remaining ingredients and have them ready to go as it cooks fast in the next step. Once the veggies are tender, add the chili powder, cumin, and oregano, and stir continuously for about 30 seconds or until fragrant and the spices soak up any remaining moisture.

3. Add the corn, lime juice, remaining ¼ teaspoon salt, and cilantro, if desired. Stir well, and cook for about 5 minutes just to heat through the corn, stirring often. Serve immediately. Garnish with cilantro and lime wedges, if desired.

· · · · · · · · · · ·

Nutrition per serving: 93 calories | 0.8g fat | 3.1g protein | 21.1g carbs | 3.3g fiber | 5.2g sugar | 442mg sodium

· · · · · · · · · · ·

⇒ *tip* ⇐

Make sure you use a mild American chili powder, which is a blend of different spices (see page 16 for more information about why this is important). If you cannot find one, then make my DIY blend on page 245.

PREP: 15 minutes
COOK: 14 minutes
YIELDS: 4 servings

· · · · · · · · · · · · · · · · ·

1 packed cup (160g) diced red onion
1 large red bell pepper, diced (160g)
1 fresh jalapeño (32g), finely diced, seeds and stems removed
¾ teaspoon (5g) fine salt, separated
¼ teaspoon (1g) ground black pepper
½ tablespoon (4g) mild chili powder or DIY Homemade Chili Powder (page 245)
1 teaspoon (3g) ground cumin
1 teaspoon (1g) dried oregano
2 cups (272g) frozen sweet corn
½ tablespoon (8g) fresh lime juice

OPTIONAL: ¼ to ½ cup (5 to 10g) roughly chopped fresh cilantro and cilantro sprigs, lime wedges for garnish

CHILI-LIME BLACK BEANS AND CORN

PREP: 5 minutes
COOK: 6 minutes
YIELDS: 3 cups

. . . .

2 (15-ounce) cans low-sodium
    black beans, drained and rinsed,
    or 3 cups cooked (510g)

½ cup (75g) frozen sweet corn

1 to 2 tablespoons (15 to 30g)
    fresh lime juice

2 teaspoons (4g) mild chili powder
    or DIY Homemade Chili
    Powder (page 245)

1 teaspoon (2g) ground cumin

1 teaspoon (1g) dried oregano

1 teaspoon (6g) fine salt

¼ to ½ teaspoon (0.5g to 1g)
    red pepper flakes

¼ teaspoon (1g) ground black
    pepper

¼ lightly filled cup (7g) fresh
    cilantro leaves

My love for chili powder and red pepper flakes was the inspiration for this side dish. Adding both to these beans and corn with a good dose of lime juice makes them full of flavor and a great side to tacos, burritos, or veggie/bean burgers. For the lime juice, I found 1 tablespoon to be enough for me, but add 2 for a more assertive lime flavor. Also, feel free to adjust the red pepper flakes depending on the spice level you can handle. If you can't find low-sodium beans, just use less salt.

Add ¼ cup (60g) water, black beans, corn, lime juice, chili powder, cumin, oregano, salt, red pepper flakes, and pepper to a medium pot over medium-low heat. Stir well, and heat through for about 5 minutes until thickened. Add the cilantro, and heat through for 1 more minute. Taste and add more salt or lime juice, if desired.

. . . .

Nutrition per ½ cup: 127 calories | 0.7g fat | 8.1g protein | 28g carbs | 7g fiber | 1.4g sugar | 546mg sodium

. . . .

❧ *tip* ❧

If you are not a fan of cilantro, then sub with fresh chopped green onions instead. Make sure you are using a mild American chili powder or use my DIY blend on page 245.

oil free • gluten free • nut free

ROASTED GOLD POTATOES WITH ROSEMARY SAUCE

I'm a self-professed herb addict, specifically rosemary. Here, I combine my favorite food—potatoes—with a creamy, thick sauce featuring one of my favorite herbs. The result: the perfect side dish to pretty much any meal. This is ideal for Thanksgiving but also works as an easy side to a lentil loaf, biscuits, or any veggie. If you don't love rosemary as much as I do, you can sub with any herb you like.

1. Preheat the oven to 400°F (200°C). Line a sheet pan with parchment paper.

2. Add the potatoes to the prepared pan, and spread out evenly in a single layer. Bake at 400°F for 15 minutes. Remove the pan from the oven, and stir the potatoes around so they cook evenly.

3. Turn up the heat to 425°F (220°C), and place the pan back in the oven to roast the potatoes for 15 to 20 more minutes or until they are well browned and tender.

4. Meanwhile, add the milk and remaining ingredients to a large deep pan, and whisk until smooth. Don't heat them just yet.

5. Once the potatoes are done, let them cool about 10 minutes to firm up before adding them to the sauce. This helps prevent them from breaking easily.

6. Once the potatoes have cooled, add them to the sauce in the pan, and turn the heat to medium-low. Cook for 3 to 5 minutes or until the sauce begins to thicken. Once it starts to thicken, it will happen rather quickly. You don't want to overcook it, but it should be thick enough to coat the back of a spoon and should not be soupy. Taste and add more salt, if desired. Serve immediately.

· · · · · · · · · · ·

Nutrition per serving: 222 calories | 1.7g fat | 7.2g protein | 48.1g carbs | 3.9g fiber | 4.4g sugar | 407mg sodium

· · · · · · · · · · ·

NOTE Since a lot of creamy, plant-based milk is called for, use one that is fairly neutral in flavor so it doesn't overpower the dish. I used soy milk. If gluten isn't an issue, you can sub all-purpose flour for the brown rice flour.

PREP: 15 minutes
COOK: 40 minutes
YIELDS: 4 servings

· · · · · · · · · · · · · · · · ·

6 heaping cups peeled and chopped (914g) Yukon Gold potatoes

1½ cups (360g) creamy plant-based milk

2 tablespoons (20g) brown rice flour

1 teaspoon (4g) garlic powder

1 teaspoon (4g) onion powder

⅛ teaspoon ground nutmeg

1 tablespoon (3g) minced fresh rosemary

½ teaspoon (3g) fine salt

¼ teaspoon (1g) ground black pepper

THE BEST FLUFFY "BUTTERMILK" MASHED POTATOES

PREP: 10 minutes
COOK: 15 minutes
YIELDS: 4 servings

. . . .

2 pounds (906g) Yukon Gold potatoes (7 to 8 medium-sized potatoes)

1½ teaspoons (9g) fine salt, separated

1½ teaspoons (6g) garlic powder, separated

½ cup (120g) canned "lite" coconut milk

1 teaspoon (5g) apple cider vinegar

¼ teaspoon (1g) ground black pepper

OPTIONAL: fresh or dried chopped thyme for garnish

Yes, "the best" is quite the claim, but it's not just me who says it. Everybody else who has made them—including many blog readers—agrees, making me confident that name is accurate. The secrets behind the best mashed potatoes I've ever eaten are the Yukon Gold potatoes, "lite" coconut milk, and garlic powder. You can use half of the garlic powder if you prefer a mild garlic taste.

1. Peel and chop the potatoes into ½-inch chunks. Add them to a large pot with 6 cups (1,440g) water, and bring to a boil over high heat. Once boiling, add 1 teaspoon salt and 1 teaspoon garlic powder, and give it a quick stir. This step really seasons the water, giving the potatoes a greater depth of flavor.

2. Lower the heat to medium-high. Cook for about 15 minutes or until the potatoes are fork-tender. Drain and let sit for 5 minutes to release some of the water.

3. Meanwhile, add the coconut milk and vinegar to a cup, and stir. Let sit for a few minutes. This creates the "buttermilk" flavor.

4. Add the remaining ½ teaspoon salt, the remaining ½ teaspoon garlic powder, and pepper to the "buttermilk," and stir.

5. Add the potatoes to a large serving bowl, and mash with a potato masher to break them up. Add the "buttermilk" and mash again until very smooth or until desired consistency is reached. If you want yours less fluffy and more creamy, add more milk, but you'll also need more spice. Taste and add more salt or spices, if desired. Garnish with thyme, if desired.

. . . .

Nutrition per ¾ cup: 172 calories | 1.9g fat | 3.5g protein | 37.3g carbs | 6.5g fiber | 3.4g sugar | 206mg sodium

. . . .

➤ *tip* ❧

"Lite" canned coconut milk will yield the very best results taste- and texture-wise in these potatoes. It creates a buttery flavor like no other milk, without any hint of coconut, and the creamiest texture. If you need a sub for the coconut milk, the next best choice is cashew milk. I wouldn't advise using any other milk, though. They just don't work as well.

SWEET POTATO CORNBREAD

I love taking classic dishes and giving them a twist. Since there are enough traditional cornbread recipes out there to pick from, I decided a version with sweet potato would be a nice partner for many of the soups and stews in this book. Plus, not only does the sweet potato provide natural sweetness, it also adds a lot of needed moisture to this oil-free cornbread. If you prefer a sweeter cornbread, be sure to stir in the optional coconut sugar.

1. Preheat the oven to 400°F (200°C). Spray an 8-inch square baking dish with nonstick spray.

2. Add the sweet potato, milk, syrup, and vinegar to a blender or food processor; process for 30 seconds or until the potato is completely smooth and frothy.

3. Add the cornmeal, oat flour, baking powder, baking soda, salt, and, if desired, sugar to a large bowl, and whisk well.

4. Pour the sweet potato mixture from the blender or food processor over the dry ingredients, and whisk until completely smooth. The batter will be on the runny side. Pour the batter into the prepared pan. Bake at 400°F on the middle rack for 25 to 27 minutes or until the top is warm golden brown, the edges have pulled away from the sides of the pan, and a toothpick inserted in the center comes out completely clean. Cool at least 30 minutes but preferably 1 hour. It will fall apart if you cut it too soon. Slice carefully and serve alongside soup or stew or with vegan butter or syrup.

. . . .

Nutrition per square: 84 calories | 1.4g fat | 2.4g protein | 15.6g carbs | 2.2g fiber | 3.7g sugar | 205mg sodium

. . . .

NOTE Microwaving or baking the sweet potato is recommended, as boiling/steaming will add too much moisture to the cornbread and yield a more dense result. To microwave, wrap a medium whole potato in plastic wrap and cook at HIGH for 5 to 6 minutes or until really soft. It keeps the potato really moist this way and the skin is being peeled anyway, so the plastic doesn't touch the part you eat. Peel and mash the potato. The soy milk is crucial to this recipe because it has a high protein content, which provides structure to the cornbread in the absence of eggs. I don't recommend using coconut milk and almond milk; the results were very crumbly and dense. If you are allergic to soy, I'd suggest using cashew milk because it has a similar fat content, but keep in mind the cornbread may be more fragile so make sure to let it cool before slicing. If you're not gluten free, you can also sub all-purpose flour for the oat flour.

PREP: 15 minutes
COOK: 25 minutes
YIELDS: 16 squares

. . . .

½ cup (120g) cooked, mashed sweet potato

1¾ cups (420g) soy milk

4 tablespoons (80g) pure maple syrup

4 teaspoons (20g) apple cider vinegar

1 cup + 2 tablespoons (188g) fine cornmeal

¾ cup (96g) gluten-free fine oat flour

1 teaspoon (6g) baking powder

1 teaspoon (6g) baking soda

½ teaspoon (3g) fine salt

2 tablespoons (20g) coconut sugar (optional)

FOOL 'EM "CREAM CHEESE" SPINACH-ARTICHOKE DIP

PREP: 20 minutes
COOK: 40 minutes
YIELDS: 6 servings

. . . .

½ cup (80g) finely diced yellow onion

3 large garlic cloves, minced (10g)

10 ounces fresh spinach, chopped into smaller pieces

1 (14-ounce) can artichoke hearts, drained well

1 cup (240g) plain, unsweetened dairy-free yogurt

1½ tablespoons (23g) distilled white vinegar

½ cup (75g) raw, unsalted cashews

½ teaspoon (3g) fine salt

½ teaspoon (2g) ground black pepper

½ packed cup (110g) cooked, peeled Yukon Gold potato

OPTIONAL: red pepper flakes for garnish, pita chips or veggies for serving

❧ tip ❧

For the yogurt, the So Delicious brand makes a plain coconut "unsweetened" that also works well. Do not use a low-fat or almond yogurt. To make this nut free, sub the cashews for ½ cup (96g) white cannellini beans. The results won't be quite as rich and creamy, so I only recommend this if you are allergic to nuts.

Aside from the dessert chapter, this is probably my favorite recipe in the whole book. I appropriately named this dish "fool 'em" because, honestly, if I hadn't created it myself, I would *swear* somebody was trying to trick me into eating dairy. For this recipe, be sure to use fresh spinach. Frozen will release way too much water and make the dip runny and bland.

1. Add the onion, garlic, and 5 tablespoons (75g) water to a small pan over medium-low heat. Bring to a simmer, and cook 5 to 8 minutes or until tender, stirring occasionally.

2. Add the spinach to the pan in small batches, stirring and tossing the spinach until it is well cooked and wilted before adding the next batch. Repeat until all the spinach is cooked well. This will take about 10 minutes. Turn the heat off.

3. Preheat the oven to 375°F (190°C).

4. Roughly chop the artichokes into quarters. This will release *lots* of liquid, so drain the excess. Squeeze out the excess liquid from the artichokes into the sink. You don't have to be obsessive about every drop, but give them a good squeeze so the dip doesn't end up watery. Add the artichokes to the cooked spinach mixture, and set aside.

5. Add the yogurt, vinegar, cashews, salt, and pepper to a high-powered blender or food processor (see Note). Add the potato to the blender; blend on high until completely smooth. Scrape the sides if needed, and blend once more. Pour over the spinach and artichoke mixture, and stir to combine everything well.

6. Pour the mixture into a 9-inch cast-iron skillet, pie dish, or an 8-inch square baking dish. Bake at 375°F for 25 minutes or until the top looks firm and set and is bubbly. Let cool for 5 to 10 minutes. For a kick, add some red pepper flakes on top before serving with pita chips or veggies.

. . . .

Nutrition per serving: 159 calories | 6.9g fat | 6.9g protein | 20.5g carbs | 4g fiber | 3g sugar | 642mg sodium

. . . .

NOTE If you do not have a high-powered blender like a Vitamix, you'll need to soak your cashews in warm water overnight, and then drain, rinse, and proceed with the recipe. Otherwise, the dip will be gritty. If using soaked cashews, I find a food processor works better than a regular, non-high-powered blender. Alternatively, you can sub with ¼ heaping cup raw cashew butter (75g) to ensure it's 100% smooth. Make sure to use a raw, no-oil-added cashew butter or make my homemade cashew butter on page 247.

SMOKY BBQ LENTIL DIP

I love barbecue anything. It is one of my favorite flavor profiles and, when paired with protein-packed lentils, makes a satisfying dip. The bold flavor makes it a good party option that both vegans and meat eaters will love. If you need less heat, use just 1 tablespoon of Sriracha.

1. Add the lentils to a food processor, but do not process yet.

2. Add the onion, garlic, and 5 tablespoons (75g) water to a small pan over medium-low heat. Bring to a simmer, and cook 5 to 8 minutes or until tender, stirring occasionally. Add a touch more water, if needed, to prevent burning, but all the water should be gone before the next step.

3. Add the cooked onions and garlic, balsamic vinegar, and remaining ingredients to the food processor; process for 2 minutes or until completely smooth. It is so delicious right away, but the flavor will intensify further overnight in the fridge and it will thicken slightly. To serve, garnish with fresh green onions, if desired, and serve with chips or veggies.

. . . .

Nutrition per ½ cup: 134 calories | 0.2g fat | 8.9g protein | 7.8g carbs | 10g fiber | 6.7g sugar | 545mg sodium

. . . .

NOTE Opt for red onion over white or yellow in this recipe. Red onion is sweeter, which complements the barbecue flavor much better.

PREP: 15 minutes
COOK: 5 minutes
YIELDS: about 3 cups

. . . .

2 (15-ounce) cans lentils, drained, rinsed, and patted dry, or 3 cups cooked lentils (510g)

½ packed cup (80g) finely chopped red onion

3 large garlic cloves, minced (15g; about 1 tablespoon)

1 tablespoon (15g) dark balsamic vinegar

5 tablespoons (75g) tomato paste

1 to 1½ tablespoons (15 to 23g) Sriracha sauce

1 tablespoon (20g) pure maple syrup

1½ teaspoons (4g) smoked paprika

1 teaspoon (6g) fine salt

OPTIONAL: ¼ cup (20g) chopped fresh green onions for garnish, potato chips or veggies for serving

THAI RED CURRY SWEET POTATO DIP

PREP: 15 minutes
COOK: 5 minutes
YIELDS: about 3 cups

. . . .

1 packed cup (248g) cooked, mashed sweet potato

1 (15-ounce) can white cannellini beans, drained and rinsed, or 1½ cups cooked white beans (255g)

2 tablespoons (30g) fresh lime juice

2 tablespoons (32g) roasted almond butter

2 tablespoons (30g) low-sodium soy sauce

¼ cup (60g) Thai red curry paste

1 teaspoon (1g) dried basil

½ teaspoon (1g) ground coriander

¼ teaspoon (2g) fine salt

OPTIONAL: roasted sliced almonds, fresh chopped basil for garnish; crackers, chips, or sliced vegetables for serving

If there was ever a dip that won over taste testers, this is it! One of my tricks for super-creamy bean dips is to use white beans, which create a really smooth dip—a big help for oil-free recipes. This dip is creamy like a hummus with bold Thai curry flavors that complement the sweet potato beautifully. With the garnishes, it makes a lovely presentation for a gathering.

Add the mashed sweet potato, beans, lime juice, almond butter, soy sauce, 2 tablespoons (30g) hot water, curry paste, basil, coriander, and salt to a food processor; process for 3 to 4 minutes or until very smooth. Scrape the sides and process again. Taste and add more salt, if desired. Garnish with almonds and basil, if desired, and serve with chips, crackers, or assorted sliced vegetables.

. . . .

Nutrition per ½ cup: 151 calories | 3g fat | 6.8g protein | 24.7g carbs | 5.4g fiber | 3.8g sugar | 704mg sodium

. . . .

NOTE Cook the sweet potato (whole with skin) either in a microwave at HIGH for 5 to 6 minutes (wrapped in plastic wrap) until very tender or bake it at 400°F (200°C) for 45 minutes to an hour until very soft. I would advise against steaming or boiling, as it will add extra water to the potatoes and dilute the flavor. Peel and mash 1 cup (248g) of the cooked potatoes. The roasted almond butter is slightly sweet, which complements the spicy curry flavor well, but if you're allergic, you can sub with tahini for a slightly different flavor profile than the original recipe.

RED PEPPER PARTY PIZZA DIP

This dip is the result of my love for roasted red peppers and pizza sauce. When you combine those two flavors, it is the perfect appetizer dip to have at a gathering. Serve this with chips or as a spread for toast.

1. Preheat the oven to 425°F (220°C). Line a large sheet pan with foil.

2. Add the whole bell pepper to the pan, and roast at 425°F for 20 to 25 minutes, rotating halfway through, until well charred.

3. Meanwhile, add the beans, tomato paste, lemon juice, Italian seasoning, garlic powder, basil, red pepper flakes, and salt to a food processor.

4. Once the bell pepper is done, carefully remove the stem and seeds, and add the pepper to the food processor. Process for 3 to 4 minutes or until completely smooth, stopping to scrape the sides a couple of times during processing. Taste and add more salt or lemon juice, if a stronger tang is desired. To serve, garnish with extra basil leaves, red pepper flakes, and black olives, if desired.

· · · · · · · · · · ·

Nutrition per ¼ cup: 68 calories | 0.2g fat | 4.5g protein | 12.9g carbs | 3.7g fiber | 3.1g sugar | 417mg sodium

· · · · · · · · · · ·

➤ tip ➤

If you cannot find the Italian seasoning, sub with 1¾ teaspoons dried oregano, ½ teaspoon dried thyme, ½ teaspoon dried basil, and ¼ teaspoon dried rosemary. Navy or Great Northern beans will also work here, but I don't recommend subbing with chickpeas.

PREP: 10 minutes
COOK: 20 minutes
YIELDS: 1¾ cups

· · · · · · · · · · · · · · · · ·

1 large red bell pepper, roughly chopped (190g)

1 (15-ounce) can low-sodium cannellini beans, drained and rinsed, or 1½ cups cooked beans (255g)

¼ cup (60g) tomato paste

1 tablespoon (15g) fresh lemon juice

1 tablespoon (3g) Italian seasoning

½ teaspoon (2g) garlic powder

15 fresh large basil leaves (5g)

½ teaspoon (1g) red pepper flakes

¾ teaspoon (5g) fine salt

OPTIONAL: basil leaves, red pepper flakes, sliced black olives for serving

SAVE THE DAY CHILI CON QUESO

PREP: 10 minutes
COOK: 5 minutes
YIELDS: about 2 cups

. . . .

¾ cup (192g) raw cashew butter or Homemade Cashew Butter (page 247)

¾ cup (180g) medium-heat smooth salsa

1 tablespoon (15g) apple cider vinegar

1 tablespoon (8g) mild chili powder or DIY Homemade Chili Powder (page 245)

½ tablespoon (7g) fresh lemon juice

½ tablespoon (4g) ground cumin

½ tablespoon (4g) paprika

¾ teaspoon (5g) fine salt

1 heaping cup (200g) canned low-sodium pinto beans, drained, or cooked pinto beans

We all need those recipes that are tasty, almost effortless to prepare, and please a crowd. When we are running behind and need a last-minute recipe for a party or gathering, this one truly does save the day. It comes together in about 15 minutes and is so incredibly hearty and rich that it does not taste like it took just minutes to prepare. I make my own raw cashew butter for my recipes since most store-bought versions have added oils, salt, or sugar and are not recommended. Turn to page 247 to see how to easily make your own.

1. Add the cashew butter, salsa, 6 tablespoons (90g) water, vinegar, chili powder, lemon juice, cumin, paprika, and salt to a small pot, and whisk well until completely smooth. Stir in the beans.

2. Turn the heat to medium-low, and bring to a low simmer. Stir continuously for 3 to 5 minutes. Continually scrape the bottom and sides of the pot to prevent sticking. This doesn't need to cook long, just enough to heat it through and thicken slightly. It thickens fast, so don't walk away. Serve immediately. Just like with regular cheese, as it sits, it will form a skin on the top, so just stir it periodically. For leftovers, just reheat in a pot on low heat. I do not recommend heating it in the microwave, as it negatively affects the texture.

. . . .
Nutrition per ½ cup: 151 calories | 3g fat | 6.8g protein | 24.7g carbs | 5.4g fiber | 3.8g sugar | 704mg sodium
. . . .

❧ tip ❧

Please keep in mind to use a salsa that you love since it contributes significantly to the flavor. Be sure to use a runny—not chunky—variety. This helps the queso mix together smoothly. Regular medium Pace Picante Sauce will do just fine here. Also, make sure you are using a mild American chili powder, which is a blend of different spices. If you cannot find one, then make my DIY blend on page 245.

CROWD-PLEASING DESSERTS

Welcome to my favorite chapter! There is absolutely nothing I enjoy more than creating and baking amazing desserts that anybody—non-vegans included—will love. Most of my recipes are gluten free, but that's simply because I prefer the taste and texture that gluten-free flours create.

My focus is very serious when it comes to dessert and my chocolate addiction is quite obvious, too! While I choose healthier ingredients and make all my desserts without any added oils, the taste will stand up to any traditional dessert—guaranteed. One request: Please use a scale with this chapter. Baking is a science and it can easily be disastrous if ingredients are measured wrong. Low amounts like teaspoons are best done with measuring spoons, but anything a tablespoon or larger is best done using the scale.

SHOWSTOPPER CHOCOLATE CAKE

PREP: 20 minutes
BAKE: 30 minutes
CHILL: 30 minutes
YIELDS: 16 servings

. . . .

1½ cups (192g) whole-wheat pastry flour or all-purpose flour

1½ teaspoons (9g) baking soda

½ teaspoon (3g) fine salt

1¼ cups (300g) dairy-free semisweet chocolate chips, separated

1¼ cups + 6 tablespoons (390g) soy milk or other creamy dairy-free milk, separated

½ cup (48g) natural unsweetened cocoa powder

1¼ cups (240g) coconut sugar

½ cup (120g) soy vanilla dairy-free yogurt

OPTIONAL: shaved dairy-free chocolate curls

➤ *tip* ◄

To make this gluten free, sub the flour with superfine oat flour (192g), add 2 tablespoons (16g) cornstarch, increase the baking soda to 2 teaspoons (12g), and decrease the milk to 1 cup (240g). All else remains the same. For the milk, you can also use cashew or almond milk, but the cake will not be nut free. For the yogurt, avoid low-fat versions or the cake will not be moist and tender. Plain will also work if you can't find vanilla.

This is the chocolate cake to whip out to wow guests. I wanted it to be the best cake I'd ever eaten. Even without eggs or oil, it tastes every bit as heavenly as a traditional chocolate cake. It has a rich, decadent, and true chocolate flavor, not just some overly sugary brown bread. It is super moist, hearty, slightly dense, yet soft. Everything a chocolate cake should be. You can make this cake the day before a party, if needed. Leave in the pan and cover tightly with foil. Store at room temperature. Slice just before serving.

1. Preheat the oven to 350°F (177°C). Line an 8-inch square aluminum pan with parchment paper cut and fitted to lie flat going both directions with a slight overhang. I advise against using dark metal pans as the sides of the cake tend to burn. Aluminum is best. If you use stoneware or ceramic, it may take slightly longer to bake through in the center. Be sure to follow the exact order for how the ingredients are mixed in. This will ensure a very moist and balanced cake.

2. To make the cake, add the flour, baking soda, and salt to a large bowl, and whisk well. Set aside.

3. Add ¼ cup (60g) chocolate chips and 1¼ cups (300g) milk to another large microwave-safe bowl, and heat in the microwave on HIGH for 30 seconds. Stir and heat for 30 more seconds, and then whisk until the chocolate is melted. Whisk in the cocoa powder until 100% smooth and no lumps remain. Add the sugar and yogurt, and whisk again.

4. Add the flour mixture in thirds to the chocolate mixture, whisking each addition in gently. Whisk until smooth and just combined with no more visible flour. Don't overmix. Pour the batter into the prepared pan. Give it a shake to even out the top.

5. Bake at 350°F on the middle rack for 30 to 35 minutes or until a toothpick inserted in the center comes out clean. Cool in the pan completely before adding the ganache, 1 to 1½ hours. The top will flatten back out as it cools.

6. To make the ganache, add 1 cup (240g) chocolate chips and 6 tablespoons (90g) milk to a microwave-safe bowl, and heat in the microwave on HIGH for 30 seconds. Stir and heat 15 to 30 more seconds, and then whisk until smooth and melted. Pour the ganache over the top of the cooled cake. Place in the fridge to firm up for 30 minutes to an hour. Carefully lift the cake out of the pan using the paper flaps. Top with shaved chocolate curls, if desired. Use a very sharp knife to slice and serve. Tightly seal leftovers with foil to keep moist.

. . . .

Nutrition per serving: 226 calories | 7.5g fat | 4.1g protein | 39.1g carbs | 3.6g fiber | 25.3g sugar | 205mg sodium

. . . .

oil free

TOFFEE-PECAN GLAZED CAKE

This cake is seriously one of the easiest cakes you'll ever make. It is super soft, light, tender, and has a wonderful toffee flavor thanks to coconut sugar and a touch of molasses. Please use a scale for accuracy, especially for cakes.

1. Preheat the oven to 350°F (177°C). Grease and flour a 9-inch cake pan. Tap the pan upside down over the sink to get rid of any excess flour. Place a round piece of parchment paper on the bottom of the pan.

2. Add the flour, ¾ cup (120g) coconut sugar, 2 tablespoons (16g) cornstarch, baking powder, and salt to a large bowl; whisk well. Pour 1¼ cups (300g) milk, ½ tablespoon (10g) molasses, and 1½ teaspoons (8g) vanilla over the flour mixture; whisk until smooth. Don't overmix. Bake at 350°F for 25 minutes or until a toothpick inserted in the center comes out clean. The cake should have a smooth, slightly domed top, and the edges will have pulled away from the pan. Cool in the pan at least 30 minutes and then flip over carefully onto a cooling rack. Let cool completely.

3. Meanwhile, decrease the oven temperature to 300°F (148°C).

4. Add the pecans to a small pan, and roast at 300°F for 5 minutes or until toasted. Be careful not to burn them.

5. To make the glaze, add ¼ cup (60g) coconut milk, 1 tablespoon (15g) water, ¼ cup (40g) coconut sugar, ¼ teaspoon (2g) molasses, and remaining ½ teaspoon (2g) cornstarch to a small pot and whisk well for 1 to 2 minutes until there are no lumps remaining. If you cannot get it smooth, strain it through a fine wire-mesh strainer to catch any unmixed lumps. Turn the heat to medium and bring to a simmer. Whisk constantly for about 1 to 2 minutes until just slightly thickened. You don't want to overcook it as it will get too thick and be hard to glaze the cake. Whisk in the remaining ¼ teaspoon vanilla. Pour the glaze over the center of the cake and use a knife or spatula to smooth the top, letting the glaze drip down the sides. Top with the roasted pecans, and serve. Store the cake in the fridge, covered, for up to 7 days. It is delicious cold as well.

. . . .

Nutrition per serving: 265 calories | 8.7g fat | 3.9g protein | 44.7g carbs | 3.4g fiber | 21.2g sugar | 165mg sodium

. . . .

NOTE Whole-wheat pastry flour is not the same as whole-wheat flour, which would make the cake too tough. The only fat in this cake is from the "lite" coconut milk, so it's vital not to sub it since it provides incredible moisture. Other milks will not be creamy enough and will not lend a light result. It's best to avoid full-fat coconut milk, too—it is way too thick and does not provide enough liquid for the batter, which will make the cake too dense. For a nut-free version, you can simply omit the pecans.

PREP: 15 minutes
BAKE: 28 minutes
YIELDS: 8 servings

. . . .

1½ cups (192g) whole-wheat pastry flour or all-purpose flour

1 cup (160g) coconut sugar, separated

2 tablespoons + ½ teaspoon (18g) cornstarch, separated

2½ teaspoons (12g) baking powder

½ teaspoon (3g) fine salt

1½ cups (360g) canned "lite" coconut milk, shaken first, separated

½ tablespoon + ¼ teaspoon (12g) unsulphured regular molasses, separated

1¾ teaspoons (9g) vanilla extract, separated

½ cup (67g) pecan halves

NO-BAKE CHOCOLATE ESPRESSO FUDGE CAKE

PREP: 15 minutes
CHILL: 2 to 4 hours or overnight
YIELDS: 6 servings

. . . .

For the crust
1 cup (140g) raw, unsalted
    sunflower seed kernels
⅛ teaspoon fine salt
2 tablespoons (12g) unsweetened
    cocoa powder
¼ teaspoon ground espresso
2½ tablespoons (50g) pure
    maple syrup

For the filling
1½ cups (300g) dairy-free
    semisweet chocolate chips
½ cup + 1 tablespoon (135g) "lite"
    canned coconut milk or cashew
    milk, shaken first
3 tablespoons (48g) creamy
    roasted almond butter
1 teaspoon (5g) vanilla extract
½ to 1 tablespoon (3 to 6g)
    ground espresso
1½ tablespoons (9g)
    unsweetened cocoa powder
⅛ teaspoon fine salt

OPTIONAL: dairy-free dark
    chocolate curls for garnish

⇢ tip ⇠

To make the chocolate curls,
place a dark chocolate bar on
a microwave-safe plate and
microwave on HIGH for just a few
seconds to slightly soften it. Use
a vegetable peeler to shave the
edges and create long curls.

I wrote this recipe years ago and am finally sharing it publicly here for the first time. Hands down, this is in my top five favorite desserts that I've ever created. It embodies everything I love in a dessert: rich chocolate flavor, lots of espresso, and the creamiest, smoothest fudge texture. Plus, it is super easy to make. For the filling, it is important to weigh the chocolate chips to ensure it sets. Feel free to adjust the espresso depending on how strong you like it. To make a larger cake, double the recipe and use a 9-inch round pan. Just note that chilling may take longer.

1. To make the crust, add the sunflower seed kernels to a food processor, and process for about 30 seconds or until finely ground into a flour. Add the salt, cocoa powder, and espresso, and process just until combined. Add the syrup, and pulse until it all comes together into sticky large clumps and holds together when pressed between your fingers.

2. Line the bottom of a 6-inch springform pan with parchment paper and spray the sides with nonstick spray for easy removal later. Press the crust mixture into the pan, making a flat, even layer along the bottom but not up the sides. Wipe your processor completely clean.

3. To make the filling, add the chocolate chips and milk to a large microwave-safe bowl. Microwave on HIGH for 30 seconds. Stir well, and then heat in 15-second increments until the chocolate is almost all melted. Stir until completely smooth and no more bits remain. Add the chocolate mixture to the food processor. Add the almond butter, vanilla, espresso, cocoa powder, and ⅛ teaspoon salt to the food processor, and process for 2 to 3 minutes or until completely smooth. Scrape the sides, and process once more.

4. Pour the filling over the crust, and smooth the top. Chill in the fridge until completely solid throughout, at least 2 to 4 hours but ideally overnight. Garnish with thickly shaved chocolate curls, if desired. (See the tip for how-to information.) Store covered in the fridge.

. . . .

Nutrition per serving: 467 calories | 32.6g fat | 8.7g protein | 43.2g carbs | 7.7g fiber | 28.4g sugar | 106mg sodium

. . . .

NOTE Cashew butter will work in place of the almond butter, just make sure it is the raw variety with no added oils or sugar. To make this nut free, sub with sunflower seed butter (such as SunButter). Thanks to all the chocolate and since it's a small amount, the sunflower seed taste is not noticeable.

ALMOND BUTTER–CHOCOLATE CHIP MUFFINS

Two of the most used ingredients in my pantry, especially for baking, are almond butter and oat flour. I love the natural health benefits of oat flour, but since it can be dense, adding starch helps to yield a soft, fluffy muffin. When you add roasted almond butter, yogurt, and chocolate chips to that blend, you have yourself one absolutely stellar muffin! You can sprinkle the muffins with additional chocolate chips before they go into the oven for a pretty presentation, if you like. Make sure all of your ingredients are at room temperature. This will ensure a smooth batter and fluffier muffin. As always, I recommend a scale for baking for accuracy. I also like to use an ice-cream scoop for perfectly shaped and high-domed muffins.

1. Preheat the oven to 350°F (177°C). Spray a 12-cup muffin pan with nonstick spray or line with parchment paper or foil liners.

2. Add the oat flour, starch, baking soda, and salt to a large bowl, and whisk very well until thoroughly combined. Stir in the chocolate chips.

3. Add the syrup, yogurt, 6 tablespoons (90g) water, almond butter, and vanilla to a medium bowl, and whisk until smooth. Pour the wet ingredients over the dry ingredients, and stir gently until just combined, being careful not to overmix. Overmixing oat-based batters can make the results dense.

4. Divide the batter evenly among the 12 prepared cups. They will be filled up to the tops. Bake at 350°F for 20 minutes or until a toothpick inserted in the center comes out completely clean. Cool 15 minutes in the pan. They'll be too delicate to remove and eat right away. Store in an airtight container for a couple of days to keep them soft and moist. The fridge works, too, if you prefer them to be more firm.

Nutrition per muffin: 292 calories | 11.4g fat | 6.4g protein | 42.6g carbs | 4.4g fiber | 20g sugar | 333mg sodium

PREP: 10 minutes
BAKE: 20 minutes
YIELDS: 12 muffins

- 2 cups + 2 tablespoons (272g) gluten-free fine oat flour
- 3 tablespoons (24g) tapioca starch
- 1½ teaspoons (9g) baking soda
- ½ teaspoon (3g) fine salt
- ¾ cup (180g) dairy-free semisweet chocolate chips
- ½ cup + 2 tablespoons (200g) pure maple syrup
- 1 cup (240g) soy or coconut varilla yogurt
- 6 tablespoons (96g) roasted creamy almond butter
- 1 teaspoon (5g) vanilla extract

tip

Cornstarch can be subbed for tapioca. You can also make these with regular all-purpose flour. Just omit the tapioca starch and use 2¼ cups (288g) all-purpose flour. Bake for 20 to 22 minutes until the tops are very golden brown and a toothpick comes out clean. For the yogurt, be sure you do not use a low-fat version. To make these nut free, sub the almond butter with sunflower seed butter if you don't mind a slight sunflower seed flavor.

BAKED PUMPKIN SPICE–CHOCOLATE CHIP DONUTS

PREP: 15 minutes
BAKE: 15 minutes
YIELDS: 6 donuts

. . . .

1¼ cups (160g) spelt flour
2 tablespoons (16g) cornstarch
2½ teaspoons (7g) Pumpkin Pie
    Spice Blend (page 238) or
    store-bought
1½ teaspoons (9g) baking powder
½ teaspoon (3g) fine salt
½ cup + 1 tablespoon (180g) pure
    maple syrup
½ cup (120g) pumpkin puree
¼ cup (60g) vanilla dairy-free
    yogurt, room temperature
6 tablespoons (90g) dairy-free
    semisweet chocolate chips

Just because you crave a donut doesn't mean you need to resort to a greasy, fried one. Sure, those taste good but they are not the healthiest choice. These pumpkin spice ones are fluffy, moist, and super soft.

1. Preheat the oven to 350°F (177°C). Spray a regular-size 6-donut pan with nonstick spray. You can also make these in a regular-size muffin pan, which will yield 8 muffins.

2. Add the flour, cornstarch, pumpkin pie spice, baking powder, and salt to a large bowl, and whisk well. To the same bowl, add the syrup, pumpkin, yogurt, and chocolate chips. Stir the ingredients well until a smooth batter is formed. The batter will be on the thick side. Be careful not to overmix. Spoon the batter evenly into the prepared pan. Using the back of a spoon, smooth and flatten out the tops of each donut. If you don't do this, they will bake up really lumpy and ugly. If you're making muffins, I find using an ice-cream scoop gives a nice rounded top.

3. Bake at 350°F for 15 minutes or until the donuts have risen beautifully, are fluffy, have a golden-brown top, and lightly spring back when touched. Muffins may take closer to 20 minutes. Look for a clean toothpick when it's inserted in the center. Let the donuts cool in the pan for about 5 minutes and then carefully flip them over onto a cooling rack. Let them cool completely. Once cooled, store any extras in a large, sealed container or ziplock bag so they don't dry out.

. . . .

Nutrition per donut: 279 calories | 6g fat | 5.3g protein | 55g carbs | 5.1g fiber | 26.8g sugar | 169mg sodium

. . . .

NOTE Be sure to use regular spelt flour, not sprouted. To make these gluten free, you can sub the spelt flour with superfine gluten-free oat flour (160g). Please keep in mind that the oat flour does make these more dense, but the flavor is just as good. Baking times are basically the same. Check for a clean toothpick. For the yogurt, I use soy but any will work. If you can't find vanilla-flavored yogurt, add 1 teaspoon vanilla extract to the recipe.

ULTIMATE-COMFORT CHOCOLATE CHIP COOKIES

These are undoubtedly the best chocolate chip cookies I've consumed—ever. Make these for your next party, but beware, they will go fast. The combo of white rice flour and tapioca in the dough means these cookies bake up with an addicting chewy center and crispy exterior.

PREP: 10 minutes
BAKE: 18 minutes
YIELDS: 14 big cookies

. . . .

1. Add the flour, starch, baking soda, and salt to a large bowl, and whisk well. Add the cashew butter, syrup, molasses, vanilla, and chocolate chips. Stir for a couple of minutes until it forms a thick, sticky batter. The batter will seem too wet at first. If it's too sticky to roll into balls immediately, place the bowl in the fridge to chill for 15 to 30 minutes. This will vary depending on your climate.

2. Preheat the oven to 375°F (190°C). Line 2 dark metal pans with parchment paper.

3. Roll 2 tablespoons of the dough into balls, creating 14 balls total. This yields nice big cookies. Place 7 balls on each pan, spacing them 2 inches apart as they will spread a lot. Press them down to between ¼ and ½ inch thick, which will make them about 2 inches wide. Place 5 to 6 chocolate chips on the tops and sprinkle with sea salt, if desired, for a fancier presentation.

4. Bake 1 pan at a time at 375°F for just 9 minutes. This will yield a crisp exterior and fudgy center. They should have spread and puffed up nicely with some hairline cracks. Remove from the oven and cool on the pan for 10 minutes. They will be very fragile, so do not eat them until they have cooled. Transfer to a wire rack to cool completely. Keep them stored in a container to prevent drying out for up to 3 days. They will soften after several hours and overnight.

. . . .

Nutrition per cookie: 197 calories | 10.7g fat | 3.2g protein | 24g carbs | 1.4g fiber | 12.7g sugar | 115mg sodium

. . . .

NOTE If you want to make these with regular all-purpose flour, use the same weight amount. I haven't tested any other flours and cannot guarantee results. If you'd like to make your own raw cashew butter, see page 247. The molasses (not blackstrap) is a crucial ingredient needed to make the baking soda react, which causes the cookies to spread and crisp up, so don't omit!

¼ cup + 2 tablespoons (60g) white rice flour

3 tablespoons (24g) tapioca starch

¾ teaspoon (4g) baking soda

¼ teaspoon (2g) fine salt

¾ cup (192g) raw cashew butter

¼ cup + 2 tablespoons (120g) pure maple syrup

1 tablespoon (20g) unsulphured molasses

½ tablespoon (7g) vanilla extract

¾ heaping cup (180g) dairy-free semisweet chocolate chips

OPTIONAL: dairy-free semisweet choclate chips, flaked sea salt for the top

oil free • gluten free

CHOCOLATE LOVERS DOUBLE-FUDGE COOKIES

PREP: 10 minutes
BAKE: 20 minutes
YIELDS: 26 cookies

. . . .

¾ cup (120g) brown rice flour
6 tablespoons (36g) unsweetened
    natural cocoa powder, sifted
1 teaspoon (8g) baking soda
½ teaspoon (3g) fine salt
2 teaspoons (2g) ground espresso
    (optional)
½ cup + 2 tablespoons (200g)
    pure maple syrup
¼ cup (60g) unsweetened
    applesauce
1 cup (256g) creamy roasted
    almond butter
1½ teaspoons (8g) vanilla extract
¾ cup (180g) dairy-free
    semisweet chocolate chips

tip

For the applesauce, make sure to use a store-bought version and not homemade, as homemade versions tend to be too watery and will make the cookies fragile and wet. If you are allergic to nuts, you can sub the almond butter with sunflower seed butter, keeping in mind it will yield a sunflower seed taste. It is masked fairly well with all the chocolate, though.

Raise your hand if you are a chocolate lover. My hand is up. I created these cookies for those of us who have a deep love of chocolate. These cookies are soft and moist with a decadent fudgy center. The applesauce gives an extra boost of moisture and softness, while the almond butter makes them rich and fudgy. The optional espresso gives these an even richer chocolate flavor.

1. Preheat the oven to 350°F (177°C). Line 2 sheet pans with parchment paper. Note that a dark metal pan will cook the bottoms better than a light-colored or aluminum pan.

2. Add the flour, cocoa powder, baking soda, salt, and, if desired, espresso to a large bowl, and whisk very well until thoroughly mixed. Add the syrup, applesauce, almond butter, vanilla, and chocolate chips. Stir for a couple of minutes or so until it all comes together into a very sticky, thick batter.

3. Drop large spoonfuls of batter, about 2 heaping tablespoons worth, onto the prepared pans spaced 2 inches apart. Fill a small bowl with water, dampen your fingertips, and press each cookie down to ½ inch thick and shape the edges together so the cookies are round. Dip your fingers in the water as needed to finish.

4. Bake 1 pan at a time at 350°F for 10 to 12 minutes. I like mine at 10 minutes, which will result in a fudgy, soft center and slightly crisp edge. At 12 minutes, the cookies will be much crispier but can dry out more quickly. Remove from the oven and cool on the pan for 10 minutes. Transfer carefully to a wire rack to cool completely. It's important to let them cool or they can fall apart. Because of the applesauce (and no oil) in these cookies, they will soften after a few hours, but they are still delicious. These are best eaten within 24 hours, as they start to dry out by the second day.

. . . .

Nutrition per cookie: 181 calories | 10.4g fat | 3.9g protein | 21.1g carbs | 2.9g fiber | 11.8g sugar | 196mg sodium

. . . .

MY FAVORITE GINGERSNAPS

This recipe should be called Destiny Gingersnaps. Reason being, when I wrote this recipe over five years ago, my husband loved it so much that he made me swear never to post it publicly on my blog and instead save it for a future cookbook—this one. These gingersnaps have been hits at parties and as gifts, and I hope they are a hit with you, too.

1. Preheat the oven to 350°F (177°C). Line a sheet pan with parchment paper. Note that a dark metal pan will cook the bottoms better than a light-colored or aluminum pan.

2. Add the almond flour, rice flour, ginger, cinnamon, baking powder, allspice, and salt to a large bowl, and whisk very well until mixed thoroughly. Add the syrup and molasses, and stir together until a thick batter forms. I use my hands to help it come together. It should be very thick and slightly sticky but able to form into balls.

3. If using the raw sugar coating, add it to a small bowl and set aside. Scoop about 1½ tablespoons of the batter and form balls with your hands. Place the balls in the bowl of sugar, if desired, and roll the balls around until evenly coated. Place the cookies on the prepared pan 2 inches apart. Press the cookies down to about ¼-inch thickness and round out the edges.

4. Bake at 350°F for 9 to 10 minutes. At 9 minutes, the finished cookies will be soft and at 10 minutes, they will be more crispy. They will be very soft upon removing them from the oven but will firm up as they cool. Cool on the pan for 10 minutes. Transfer carefully to a wire rack to cool completely. Make sure to use a thin spatula to transfer them and not your hands because these are delicate and will fall apart. Store the cookies in an airtight container and they will stay moist for several days.

Nutrition per cookie: 148 calories | 7.9g fat | 1.4g protein | 17.7g carbs | 2g fiber | 9g sugar | 59mg sodium

PREP: 10 minutes
BAKE: 9 minutes
YIELDS: 9 cookies

- 1¼ cups (140g) superfine blanched almond flour
- ¼ cup (40g) white rice flour
- 2½ teaspoons (6g) ground ginger
- 1 teaspoon (2g) ground cinnamon
- 1 teaspoon (4g) baking powder
- ½ teaspoon ground allspice
- ¼ teaspoon (2g) fine salt
- 5 tablespoons (100g) pure maple syrup
- 2 tablespoons (30g) unsulphured molasses

OPTIONAL: ¼ cup (66g) raw sugar for coating

⇒ *tip* ⇐

Please make sure to use a superfine blanched almond flour. (See page 26 for tips on brands.) If you use a flour that's too gritty, it will make the dough more wet and yield gritty cookies. It is also important to use white rice flour for these cookies and not brown rice flour. The white rice flour has much greater binding qualities and helps the structure.

MAGICAL CHOCOLATE CHIP COOKIE BARS

PREP: 10 minutes
BAKE: 30 minutes
YIELDS: 16 bars

. . . .

½ cup + 2 tablespoons (100g) white rice flour

½ cup (96g) coconut sugar

¼ cup (32g) cornstarch

½ teaspoon (3g) fine salt

½ cup (160g) pure maple syrup

¼ cup (60g) plant-based milk

1½ teaspoons (8g) vanilla extract

1 cup (256g) creamy roasted almond butter

½ cup + 2 tablespoons (150g) dairy-free semisweet chocolate chips, separated

I honestly couldn't think of a better name for these bars other than "magical." Or perhaps I should have named them "dangerous" because, I am not going to lie, they were gone in two days. They are literally like the best chocolate chip cookie ever, but in bar form.

1. Preheat the oven to 350°F (177°C). Line an 8-inch square stoneware or ceramic pan with parchment paper cut and fitted to lie flat going both directions with a slight overhang. Metal pans tend to make the outsides burn faster because of the cornstarch.

2. Add the rice flour, coconut sugar, cornstarch, and salt to a large bowl, and whisk well. Pour in the syrup, milk, vanilla, almond butter, and only 6 tablespoons (90g) of the chocolate chips. Stir everything well until it becomes a smooth and very thick batter. Pour the batter into the prepared pan. It will be sticky. Dampen your fingers with water and smooth and press the top out evenly, making sure to press it into the corners. Go along the edges with your fingertips to flatten evenly. Top with the remaining ¼ cup (60g) chocolate chips.

3. Bake at 350°F for 30 to 35 minutes or until the top is golden brown and shiny and a toothpick inserted in the center has a few sticky crumbs but not wet batter. Remove from the oven and cool in the pan for 30 minutes—cooling is no exception here, as the bars will fall apart. Lift out the bars with the parchment paper, and cool on a wire rack for another 15 minutes, and then slice into 16 bars. I will be impressed if you don't eat them all within a day, but if you don't, you can store them for up to 3 days at room temperature covered with foil.

. . . .

Nutrition per bar: 225 calories | 11.3g fat | 4.5g protein | 28.9g carbs | 2.8g fiber | 17.2g sugar | 77mg sodium

. . . .

➤ *tip* ➤

Don't sub brown rice flour for the white rice flour. It will make the bars dry and crumbly. I use Bob's Red Mill. If you are not gluten free, you can sub with all-purpose flour, but the weight is different, 80g. You still need to use the cornstarch. For the milk, I've tested both soy and almond. To make them nut free, sub the almond butter with sunflower seed butter. Keep in mind, this will yield a strong sunflower seed taste to the bars, so it's only recommended if you are a sunflower seed butter fan.

CROWD-PLEASING BROWNIES

I write a lot of brownie recipes: Zucchini brownies, coconut brownies, white bean brownies, pumpkin brownies, and sunflower brownies are several that are found on my blog. For this book, I wanted to produce the most crowd-pleasing brownie I've created to date, something as close to a traditional brownie as possible. You know, the perfect blend of fudgy and cakey and not those sad, super-thin ones. It took me many trials, but this recipe is, to me, the most perfect brownie—crispy, chewy edges with a fudgy center.

1. Preheat the oven to 350°F (177°C). Line an 8-inch square stoneware or ceramic pan with parchment paper cut and fitted to lie flat going both directions with a slight overhang. Metal and aluminum pans tend to make the outsides burn faster because of the cornstarch.

2. Add the rice flour, cornstarch, and baking powder to a medium bowl, and whisk well. Set aside.

3. Add the almond butter, syrup, and ¼ cup (60g) water to a large bowl, and whisk until smooth. Add the coconut sugar, cocoa powder, and salt, and whisk again. Add the flour mixture and only ½ cup (120g) of the chocolate chips to the almond butter mixture, and stir until it comes together into a sticky, thick batter. Spoon the batter into the prepared pan and spread out the top. Dip your fingertips into water and flatten out the top and make sure it's evenly spread out to the corners. Top with the remaining ¼ cup (60g) chocolate chips.

4. Bake at 350°F for 35 to 40 minutes or until the top is shiny and a toothpick inserted in the center has a bit of sticky batter. It shouldn't be wet, but sticky crumbs. Start checking at 35 minutes. If you pull them out at 35 minutes, they'll still be very gooey. At 40 minutes, they'll be fudgy with chewy, crispy edges. You may need to bake them the first time to see how you prefer them, since ovens vary. If the edges are browning too much, place a piece of foil over the top. Cool in the pan for a minimum of 1 hour, no exception. They will finish cooking in the center as they cool, so resist the urge, and wait to cut them or they will be a mess.

5. Lift the brownies out of the pan with the parchment flaps and use a very sharp knife to cut them. If your edges crisped more than you like, you can trim them off. Store sealed at room temperature so they don't dry out for up to 3 days.

Nutrition per brownie: 246 calories | 12.3g fat | 5g protein | 33.1g carbs | 3.9g fiber | 19.4g sugar | 76mg sodium

PREP: 15 minutes
BAKE: 35 minutes
YIELDS: 16 brownies

. . . .

½ cup + 2 tablespoons (100g) white rice flour
¼ cup (32g) cornstarch
½ teaspoon (2g) baking powder
1 cup (256g) creamy roasted almond butter
½ cup + 2 tablespoons (200g) pure maple syrup
½ cup (96g) coconut sugar
½ cup (48g) natural unsweetened cocoa powder
½ teaspoon (3g) fine salt
½ cup (120g) dairy-free semisweet chocolate chips + ¼ cup (60g) for top, separated

tip

Don't sub brown rice flour for the white rice flour. It will make the brownies dry and crumbly. If you are not gluten free, you can sub with all-purpose flour, but use 80g; they are a tad less fudgy. You still need to use the cornstarch. For the sugar, you can sub white sugar; it will make them slightly sweeter. For the chocolate chips, I use Guittard brand regular-sized semisweet chips. This brand contains vanilla, but if yours doesn't, add ½ teaspoon vanilla extract in Step 3. Otherwise, Trader Joe's and Enjoy Life carry dairy-free chips. I prefer the larger chips rather than the mini, as they melt better and give a fudgier texture.

CHOCOLATE-PEANUT BUTTER CANDY BITES

PREP: 20 minutes
CHILL: 20 minutes
YIELDS: 8 balls

. . . .

½ cup (128g) smooth peanut
    butter
3 tablespoons (18g) unsweetened
    natural cocoa powder
3 tablespoons (60g) pure maple
    syrup
1 teaspoon (5g) vanilla extract
¼ teaspoon (2g) fine salt
½ cup (80g) roasted, salted
    peanuts
¼ cup (40g) coconut sugar
3.5 ounces (100g) 70 to
    72% dark chocolate chips
    or bar, finely chopped

❧ tip ❧

Be sure to use a peanut butter
without added oil or sugar. To make
these nut free, sub the peanut
butter with sunflower seed butter,
if you don't mind having that as a
strong taste in these bites. With
this sub, the batter may be a tad
more wet and may need to chill in
the fridge for 15 minutes before
adding the chocolate.

My favorite candy bar growing up was Butterfinger. I swear, I could eat those back to back. These bites have the same flavors of the classic candy bar but are so much better. Instead of the outside being the chocolate coating with the crunchy sweet interior, I reversed them and also made them into bites. Man, they are delicious and a favorite among my taste testers! If you can't find salted peanuts, then add a pinch of salt.

1. Line a sheet pan with parchment paper. Set aside.

2. Add the peanut butter, cocoa powder, maple syrup, vanilla, and sea salt to a bowl, and stir until it comes together into a thick batter and is completely smooth. Roll about a heaping tablespoon of the dough into small balls, creating 8 balls total. Place the balls on the prepared pan.

3. To prepare the coating, add the roasted peanuts and coconut sugar to a food processor, and process until the mixture is in very small pieces but not as superfine as a flour consistency. Add this mixture to a wide, shallow bowl. Set aside.

4. Add the chopped chocolate to another small microwave-safe bowl. Melt in the microwave on HIGH for 30 seconds or in a double boiler. If microwaving, stir, and then heat in 10- to 15-second intervals until the chocolate is almost all melted. Be careful not to let it burn. Stir the chocolate until it is completely melted and smooth.

5. Place 1 ball into the melted chocolate and use a fork to rotate and coat it completely. Tap the fork gently on the side of the bowl, letting the excess chocolate drip off. Immediately place the ball into the peanut coating mixture and rotate it multiple times with the fork until coated well. Place the ball back on the pan and repeat with the remaining balls.

6. Place the pan in the fridge to set for about 20 minutes. Store the balls in the fridge to retain their shape. They can be set out at room temperature after they're fully set for parties, but they will become softer and less crispy as time passes.

. . . .
Nutrition per ball: 260 calories | 23.2g fat | 8.7g fat | 26.3g carbs | 4g fiber | 19g sugar | 209mg sodium
. . . .

MY GO-TO PARTY TRUFFLES

I've been making truffles for years and years for guests, the holidays, and for gifts. I've made many different varieties, but these are my favorite and my go-to recipe that I'm finally sharing. I love the combo of the semisweet chocolate and cocoa powder. It provides the perfect sweetness without being too sweet or too bitter. Double the recipe if you're serving several guests. I like to do a mix of different coatings because I enjoy the taste variety and how pretty it looks on a platter at a party. Cocoa powder is my favorite, but other sugars are great for a sweet truffle, and crushed pistachios look beautiful.

1. Add the chocolate chips and milk to a medium microwave-safe bowl, and microwave on HIGH for 30 seconds. Stir the chocolate, and microwave 15 seconds more. Stir the chocolate until 100% melted and smooth.

2. Add the remaining ingredients to the melted chocolate; whisk until completely smooth with no lumps remaining from the cocoa powder. Place the bowl in the fridge until very firm and set. I suggest 4 to 8 hours minimum, but overnight is highly recommended. The longer it sits, the easier it will be to roll into balls.

3. Once the dough has chilled, place the coating options in separate bowls. Line a plate with parchment paper. Set aside.

4. Using a tablespoon or melon scooper, scoop out about a tablespoon of the dough, and roll into a ball. Place the ball into the desired coating and rotate the ball until completely coated. Place onto the prepared plate. Work quickly, as the warmth from your hands will soften the chocolate. If needed, periodically wipe off your hands with a paper towel. Repeat with the remaining dough, creating 12 truffles total. Store the truffles in the fridge until ready to serve. They will be soft but firm, and perfect to serve. If they sit out for a long time, they will soften.

Nutrition per 2 truffles: 141 calories | 9.6g fat | 2.2g protein | 16.2g carbs | 2.1g fiber | 11.9g sugar | 52mg sodium

PREP: 20 minutes
CHILL: 4 to 8 hours or overnight
YIELDS: 12 truffles

• • • • • • • • • • • • • • • • •

¾ cup (150g) dairy-free semisweet chocolate chips

3 tablespoons (45g) "lite" canned coconut milk, shaken first

½ tablespoon (8g) raw cashew butter

¼ teaspoon (3g) vanilla extract

1 tablespoon (6g) natural unsweetened cocoa powder, sifted

⅛ teaspoon fine salt

¼ teaspoon ground espresso (optional)

OPTIONAL: cocoa powder, powdered sugar, crushed nuts, for coating

NOTE For the milk, be sure not to sub with a different milk or they will not firm up. For a nut-free sub, use sunflower seed butter. I do not recommend using almond butter.

✤ tip ✤

Different chocolate brands have varying amounts of cocoa butter, which affects the texture and how hard or soft the truffles will be. I use Enjoy Life dairy-free semisweet chocolate chips for this recipe, which is about 52 to 55% cocoa. Do not use a 60% or higher chocolate, as the truffles will be too hard and bitter. Also, depending on your brand, yours may harden quicker or take longer. If the dough gets too hard to roll into balls, just set the chocolate out at room temperature to soften a bit. Don't use a milk chocolate.

WHITE CHOCOLATE–MACADAMIA COOKIE GRANOLA

PREP: 15 minutes
BAKE: 25 minutes
YIELDS: 5 cups

. . . .

½ cup (160g) pure maple syrup

¼ cup (64g) creamy roasted almond butter

2 tablespoons (40g) unsulphured molasses

½ tablespoon (8g) vanilla extract

¼ teaspoon (2g) fine salt

2½ cups (250g) gluten-free old-fashioned oats, not instant

½ cup (80g) macadamia nuts or almonds, chopped into small pieces

0.9 ounces (25g) dairy-free white chocolate bar, finely chopped

Who doesn't love the classic white chocolate macadamia nut cookies?! Well, those cookies are what inspired me to create this cookie granola that's sweet like a cookie but in granola form. I would definitely call this "special occasion granola," as it's truly more like a cookie than a healthy breakfast-style granola. Vegan white chocolate can be a bit tricky to find; I order mine online. If you like, add extra chopped white chocolate to the granola after it bakes up.

1. Preheat the oven to 325°F (165°C). Line a sheet pan with parchment paper.

2. Combine the syrup, almond butter, molasses, vanilla, and salt in a large bowl, and stir well until smooth. Add the oats, nuts, and white chocolate, and stir well until it all comes together and is very sticky.

3. Transfer the oats mixture to the prepared pan, and spread out evenly, making sure all of the granola is touching. This is important so it will form clumps as it bakes.

4. Bake at 325°F for 15 minutes. Remove the pan from the oven, and stir the granola around really well, making sure to rotate the granola from underneath. Bake 10 to 15 more minutes or until very golden brown, watching the edges closely so they don't burn.

5. Cool for 10 to 15 minutes. It will become very crispy as it cools. Store in an airtight container for up to 2 weeks.

. . . .

Nutrition per ½ cup: 251 calories | 9.4g fat | 4.1g protein | 33.1g carbs | 3.2g fiber | 13.1g sugar | 64mg sodium

. . . .

❧ *tip* ❧

To make this nut free, sub the almond butter with sunflower seed butter (such as SunButter), and omit the nuts or sub with your favorite seed. If you are not a strong macadamia nut lover, then I suggest using almonds or a combo of both, as the macadamia nut flavor comes through boldly in this granola.

CHOCOLATE FUDGE SWIRL ICE CREAM

Want to impress your dairy-loving friends and family? Then make them this ice cream and don't tell them it is dairy free. This is every bit as rich, creamy, and delicious. And the fudge swirl—watch out! I share two methods to make this ice cream: a faster one using an ice-cream maker and another that just uses your freezer. If you've got one, I recommend using an ice-cream maker, as the results are creamier.

1. Make the fudge swirl by adding only ¼ (80g) cup of the syrup, almond butter, and 1½ tablespoons of the cocoa powder to a coffee mug or cup, and whisk with a fork until completely smooth. Heat in the microwave on HIGH for 30 seconds. This is to melt the cocoa powder and cause it to slightly thicken as it cools. Whisk once more, and place in the fridge to cool and thicken.

2. Make the ice cream base by adding the raw cashews, milk, sugar, remaining 6 tablespoons cocoa powder, remaining ¼ cup syrup, vanilla, sweet potato, and salt to a high-powered blender or food processor (see tip), and blend until completely smooth. Scrape the sides and blend once more.

3. If using an ice-cream maker, transfer the ice cream base to the canister and churn the ice cream for 15 to 20 minutes or until it reaches a soft-serve texture. Pour the fudge swirl in during the last few seconds of churning just until mixed in. Do not over-churn. If not using an ice-cream maker, pour the ice cream base into a heavy, freezer-safe container with a tight-fitting lid or covered with a couple of pieces of foil, and freeze for 2 to 3 hours. It needs to reach a pudding-like or semi-firm consistency before swirling in the fudge. Otherwise, the fudge swirl will just melt into the ice cream base. Once the ice cream has reached a pudding-like texture, stir until smooth, and then drop spoonfuls of about half of the fudge on top. Gently press some of the fudge down into the middle of the ice cream and then drop the remaining fudge on top. Swirl the fudge around a tiny bit with a knife. You don't want to over-swirl it or the fudge swirls will not be as detectable in the frozen ice cream.

4. Place the swirled ice cream back in the freezer for 3 to 6 hours to freeze completely until firm and solid enough to scoop. This yields 3¼ cups of ice cream. If you freeze it overnight, take it out a few minutes before serving so that it softens a bit. The version not made with an ice-cream maker will be more icy and not nearly as creamy.

. . . .

Nutrition per serving: 347 calories | 19g fat | 8g protein | 42g carbs | 3.6g fiber | 25.2g sugar | 106mg sodium

. . . .

PREP: 15 minutes
CHILL: 5 to 9 hours
YIELDS: 7 servings

. . . .

½ cup (160g) pure maple syrup, separated
2 tablespoons (32g) creamy roasted almond butter or nut butter of choice
7½ tablespoons (45g) unsweetened natural cocoa powder, separated
1½ cups (225g) raw, unsalted cashews
2 cups (480g) canned "lite" coconut milk, shaken first
6 tablespoons (60g) coconut sugar
1½ teaspoons (8g) vanilla extract
¼ cup (60g) sweet potato puree
¼ teaspoon (2g) fine salt

⇥ *tip* ⇤

If you do not have a high-powered blender like a Vitamix, see the note on page 247 for substitutions. Alternatively, you can sub with raw cashew butter for the same amount, 225g, which is ¾ cup + 2 tablespoons. For the milk, "lite" yields the creamiest result and no coconut taste. It works best above all other milks for this. Any other subs will yield more of an icy result.

⫷⫷⫷⫷

oil free • gluten free

CHAI-SPICED ALMOND CARAMEL

PREP: 5 minutes
COOK: 4 minutes
YIELDS: ¾ cup

. . . .

½ cup (160g) pure maple syrup
¼ cup (64g) creamy roasted
    almond butter
1 tablespoon (15g) creamy
    plant-based milk
½ teaspoon (1g) ground
    cinnamon
¼ + ⅛ teaspoon ground
    cardamom
¼ teaspoon ground ginger
⅛ teaspoon ground nutmeg
Pinch of ground cloves
Pinch of ground black pepper

Another word for this caramel is addiction. Because that is, straight-up, what this became when I created it. I am a huge, I mean *huge,* chai lover. The spices and warmth just make me happy. Well, this caramel is next-level thanks to a chai spice infusion. It has a wonderful aroma, as well as an intense spice flavor that is so much better than plain caramel. It is rich, creamy, thick, and amazing on just about anything: ice cream, pancakes, brownies, bars, or even as a sweetener to liven up coffee or a latte.

1. Add all of the ingredients to a bowl, and whisk well until smooth. Add the mixture to a small pot over medium heat. Bring the mixture to a simmer, and then cook for 2 to 3 minutes, whisking constantly to prevent sticking and clumping. It should thicken up quickly. Remove from the heat.

2. Let the caramel cool for 15 minutes, as it will really thicken as it cools. If you would like it thicker, heat it for about another minute, and then repeat the cooling. Store in the fridge, and it will get even thicker. To serve, bring it back to room temperature to loosen the texture again.

. . . .
Nutrition per 2 tablespoons: 119 calories | 5.6g fat | 1.7g protein | 20g carbs | 1.2g fiber | 16.2g sugar | 3mg sodium
. . . .

NOTE To make this nut free, sub the almond butter with sunflower seed butter. Keep in mind, this will yield a sunflower seed butter taste. For the milk, I use "lite" coconut.

GINGERBREAD LATTE

If you love spicy gingerbread cake, then you will love this latte. This ultra-smooth and creamy latte has the holiday season written all over it, although you certainly can make it year-round—nobody will mind. This warm drink is spiced with ginger, cinnamon, nutmeg, cloves, and vanilla for a richly flavored and satisfying latte. Drink as is, or for a full-on latte party, top with dairy-free whipped cream (I love Lite So Delicious CocoWhip) and a sprinkle of freshly ground cinnamon. Even some candied ginger on top would be delicious if you are a huge ginger fan like I am!

1. Add the coffee, syrup, ginger, cinnamon, nutmeg, cloves, vanilla, pepper, and salt to a bowl and whisk well until smooth. Pour the coffee mixture evenly into 2 mugs.

2. Add the milk to a small pot over low heat, and heat until steamed but not boiling. Use a frother to create foam, if desired. Pour the milk evenly (1 cup per mug) over the coffee, and stir well to combine. Alternatively, if you don't care about making a latte the traditional way, just blend everything in a blender until frothy. Heat over the stove for a few minutes on low until steamed. Add toppings, if desired. Serve immediately.

Nutrition per serving: 225 calories | 12.3g fat | 3.3g protein | 31.3g carbs | 0.9g fiber | 18.1g sugar | 65mg sodium

PREP: 5 minutes
COOK: 3 minutes
YIELDS: 2 servings

¾ cup (180g) strong-brewed hot coffee

3 tablespoons (60g) pure maple syrup

1½ to 2 teaspoons (4 to 5g) ground ginger

1 teaspoon (2g) ground cinnamon

¼ teaspoon ground nutmeg

⅛ teaspoon ground cloves

¼ teaspoon (2g) vanilla extract

Pinch each of ground black pepper and fine salt

2 cups (480g) creamy plant-based milk

OPTIONAL: dairy-free whipped cream, ground cinnamon, and candied ginger, for topping

NOTE Since this is a latte, creamy milk is best. I think canned "lite" coconut milk is best for flavor and texture, and it yields no coconut taste. I would advise against almond or other "lite" milks.

10

STAPLES

This chapter is all about the recipes that I simply cannot live without. Often, what makes a meal complete is that perfect sauce or seasoning blend. I'm sharing my favorites here. These are recipes I make over and over and like to keep on hand for quick meals. A few of these are popular from my blog and some are new, but they are all good go-to options for making mealtime easy for me and, of course, for you. The sauces can be frozen, and then thawed overnight in the fridge to bring them back to life. A big perk of these recipes is that most take 10 minutes or less to make. How is that for easy?

EMERGENCY SMOKY BARBECUE SAUCE

PREP: 5 minutes
COOK: 10 minutes
YIELDS: 2 ½ cups

. . . .

2 cups (480g) tomato
 sauce/puree
4 tablespoons (80g) pure
 maple syrup
4 teaspoons (20g) liquid smoke
5 tablespoons (76g) vegan
 Worcestershire
1 teaspoon (7g) blackstrap
 molasses
1 teaspoon (4g) garlic powder
¼ teaspoon (1g) ground black
 pepper

This is a fantastic barbecue sauce that doesn't require a ton of time or ingredients to make. It has a universal flavor that's not spicy and that everybody will love. It doesn't have loads of sugar or preservatives like store-bought versions. Oh, and the flavor is amazing! It really intensifies and comes alive when heated up!

Add all of the ingredients to a food processor or blender, and blend until well mixed. Store in the fridge overnight to let the flavors develop. This step isn't crucial, but the flavor does develop more as it sits. When ready to use, add the sauce to a small pot over medium-low heat. Let it simmer about 10 minutes or until it is hot and slightly thickened. If using this sauce in a recipe, like my BBQ Sweet Potato and Bean Soup on page 149 and Ultimate BBQ Bean Ball Sub on page 138, then do not cook the sauce first.

. . . .

Nutrition per ¼ cup: 41 calories | 0.1g fat | 0.7g protein | 9.7g carbs | 0.8g fiber | 8.4g sugar | 361mg sodium

. . . .

tip

Vegan Worcestershire is a crucial ingredient affecting the flavor of the barbecue sauce, so make sure to include it! See page 18 for my brand recommendations.

SESAME TERIYAKI SAUCE

This teriyaki sauce—a longtime reader favorite—really perks up plain rice or veggies! Made with fresh ginger, garlic, chives, and toasted sesame seeds, it is so much better and fresher than commercial versions. It definitely becomes the star of any dish you serve it on! My favorite way to serve this is over brown rice, peas, and carrots, and top with extra chives and sesame seeds.

1. Add the coconut aminos, maple syrup, ¼ cup (60g) water, ginger, garlic, chives, and sesame seeds to a small pot, and whisk together well. Add the brown rice flour, whisking until there are no lumps. Add the cayenne. Turn the heat to medium, and bring to a low boil. Cook for 3 to 5 minutes or until the mixture begins to thicken, whisking around the edges a couple of times while it cooks. Be careful not to cook it too long or it will get too thick once cooled.

2. Remove from the heat, and let cool for 5 minutes. It should have a syrup consistency as it cools. If it's not a syrup consistency after a few minutes of cooling, cook just a couple more minutes. This can be frozen for up to 6 months. Thaw it in the fridge, and then reheat on low on the stove.

. . . .

Nutrition per ¼ cup: 104 calories | 0.6g fat | 0.4g protein | 23g carbs | 0.3g fiber | 12g sugar | 43mg sodium

. . . .

NOTE The coconut aminos are crucial here and cannot be subbed with liquid aminos or soy sauce, as those are way too salty. Coconut aminos are sweeter and much less salty. This can be found at many grocery stores in the same aisle as the soy sauce or also online on Amazon.

PREP: 10 minutes
COOK: 3 minutes
YIELDS: 1¼ cups

. . . .

¾ cup (180g) coconut aminos

¼ cup + 2 tablespoons (100g) pure maple syrup

½ packed tablespoon (8g) minced ginger

1 teaspoon (4g) minced garlic

1 tablespoon (3g) finely chopped fresh chives

½ tablespoon (5g) toasted sesame seeds

1 tablespoon (10g) brown rice flour

1/16 to 1/8 teaspoon cayenne pepper

EASIEST-EVER PIZZA/SPAGHETTI SAUCE

PREP: 10 minutes
YIELDS: 2 cups

. . . .

2 cups (480g) plain tomato sauce
  puree
1½ teaspoons (1g) dried oregano
1½ teaspoons (1g) dried basil
1 teaspoon (4g) onion powder
1 teaspoon (4g) garlic powder
½ teaspoon dried thyme
¼ teaspoon (1g) ground black
  pepper
1 tablespoon (20g) pure maple
  syrup
½ teaspoon (3g) fine salt

OPTIONAL: ¼ teaspoon red
  pepper flakes

Seriously, never buy jarred sauce again. My homemade version literally takes just a few minutes to put together, making it ideal as a last-minute spaghetti sauce. It is truly a staple in my home—I always keep some stored in the fridge. If you use a salt-free tomato sauce, you may need to add more salt to this sauce.

Add all of the ingredients to a blender or food processor, and blend until smooth. If using as a pizza sauce, just add it to your pre-baked pizza crust, add the toppings, and bake. If serving over pasta, simply warm it on the stove first. You can store this in the fridge for 2 weeks or the freezer for up to 3 months. Reheat over low heat on the stove. Since the sauce is oil free and made from pureed tomatoes, it will thicken up a lot in the fridge, so be sure to reheat over low heat on the stove and whisk well to bring it back to a sauce consistency.

. . . .

Nutrition per ¼ cup: 24 calories | 0.2g fat | 0.9g protein | 5.7g carbs | 1.1g fiber | 4.3g sugar | 462mg sodium

. . . .

ENCHILADA SAUCE

It is practically impossible to find a healthy, oil-free enchilada sauce on the market, but this tastier homemade version is ready in no time. Add more or less chili powder depending on your heat preference.

Add all of the ingredients and 1 cup (240g) water to a small pot, and whisk until mixed well. Turn the heat to medium-high, and, once simmering, whisk continually for 3 to 5 minutes or until the sauce has thickened some. Remove from the heat, and use as desired. You can store this in the fridge for 2 weeks or the freezer for up to 3 months. Reheat over low heat on the stove.

. . . .

Nutrition per ¼ cup: 53 calories | 1g fat | 1.2g protein | 11.4g carbs | 2.1g fiber | 5.4g sugar | 464mg sodium

. . . .

PREP: 10 minutes
COOK: 3 minutes
YIELDS: 1½ cups

. . . .

½ cup (120g) tomato sauce/ puree
2 tablespoons (18g) chili powder
1 teaspoon (4g) garlic powder
1 teaspoon (4g) onion powder
1 teaspoon (6g) fine salt
1 teaspoon (2g) ground cumin
2 tablespoons (20g) brown rice flour or all-purpose flour
2 tablespoons (40g) pure maple syrup or agave syrup

ROASTED ALMOND BUTTER

PREP: 10 minutes
COOK: 15 minutes
YIELDS: 1¾ cups

. . . .

3 cups (450g) raw, unsalted whole almonds

If you take a look at just the desserts chapter, you can get an idea of my love for almond butter. It is the perfect oil replacement in many baked goods, particularly cookies or fudgy brownies. It gives richness and depth of flavor and is a whole food, unlike processed oils. It is also delicious served on toast or in oatmeal! I have been making my own for years, and it couldn't be easier. All you need are almonds and a food processor! You'll need at least an 11-cup capacity food processor for this recipe.

1. Preheat the oven to 300°F (150°C). Line a sheet pan with parchment paper.

2. Spread out the almonds evenly on the prepared pan. Roast at 300°F for 15 minutes.

3. Add the roasted nuts to a food processor, and process for a few minutes until the nuts turn into a paste, stopping to break up the clumps several times during the process. You will need to do this quite a bit in the beginning. Process the nuts for several more minutes until silky smooth. Do not be tempted to stop when it's a thick paste, keep going, and then some more, until it is completely silky smooth and pours easily off a spoon. You will have the creamiest, silkiest nut butter ever. Let it cool before using in any recipe.

. . . .

Nutrition per tablespoon: 93 calories | 8g fat | 3.4g protein | 3.4g carbs | 2g fiber | 0.7g sugar | 0mg sodium

. . . .

variation

SWEET GINGER ALMOND BUTTER

Once you've reached the silky smooth almond butter stage, add 1 tablespoon (8g) ground cinnamon, 1 to 2 teaspoons (2 to 4g) ground ginger (to taste), ¼ cup (40g) coconut sugar, 1 teaspoon (5g) vanilla extract, and ¼ teaspoon (2g) fine salt to the almond butter; process for a minute and enjoy!

CHAI SPICE BLEND

PREP: 5 minutes
YIELDS: about 7 tablespoons

. . . .

3 tablespoons (24g) ground
   cinnamon

2 tablespoons + ¾ teaspoon (16g)
   ground cardamom

1½ tablespoons (9g) ground
   ginger

2¼ teaspoons (6g) ground
   nutmeg

¼ teaspoon ground cloves

⅛ teaspoon ground black pepper

Welcome to my favorite blend. I'm a spice lover even more than a chocolate lover, and my love for chocolate runs *deep*. The warmth and depth that comes from this combination of spices just makes me feel so good. You can use this blend to spruce up pancakes, waffles, lattes, and syrups. Heck, you can even sprinkle it over ice cream or puddings. Also, please note that grams are not given for some of the ingredients because the amounts are so low that they don't register on a scale, so using the teaspoon measure is best.

Add all of the ingredients to a small bowl, and whisk very well. Alternatively, add them to a jar with a tight-fitting lid and shake vigorously to ensure even mixing. Store in a sealed container in a cool, dry place for up to 6 months, but it probably won't last a month!

. . . .

Nutrition per tablespoon: 22 calories | 0.5g fat | 0.5g protein | 5g carbs | 2.5g fiber | 0.3g sugar | 1mg sodium

. . . .

PUMPKIN PIE SPICE BLEND

PREP: 5 minutes
YIELDS: about 10 tablespoons

. . . .

½ cup (64g) ground cinnamon
4 teaspoons (8g) ground ginger
2 teaspoons (5g) ground allspice
1 teaspoon (3g) ground nutmeg
1 teaspoon (3g) ground cloves

Although pumpkin pie spice is easy to find in the United States, it's not as common in other countries. I created this easy, fresh DIY blend for any and all recipes that call for pumpkin pie spice, such as my Baked Pumpkin Spice–Chocolate Chip Donuts on page 200 or my Pumpkin Spice, Cranberry, and Pistachio Morning Cookies on page 40. I always have this stuff on hand. I absolutely love it!

Add all of the ingredients to a small bowl, and whisk very well. Alternatively, add them to a jar with a tight-fitting lid and shake vigorously to ensure even mixing. Store in a sealed container in a cool, dry place for up to 6 months.

. . . .

Nutrition per tablespoon: 19 calories | 0.3g fat | 0.3g protein | 5.5g carbs | 3.2g fiber | 0.2g sugar | 2mg sodium

. . . .

CAJUN SPICE SEASONING

Many store blends of Cajun seasoning contain additives or salt that I don't really want, so I came up with this salt-free blend to keep in my pantry. One big benefit of this salt-free version is that you get the same flavors but can control how much sodium goes into your recipes. For a milder blend, decrease the cayenne to 1½ teaspoons. This seasoning is featured in a number of my recipes, including Cajun Veggie and Potato Chowder on page 158, Creamy Cajun Lemon Sauce on page 91, and Time-Saver Cajun Red Beans and Rice on page 122.

Add all of the ingredients to a small bowl, and whisk very well. Store the blend in a sealed jar for up to 6 months.

. . . .

Nutrition per tablespoon: 21 calories | 0.5g fat | 0.9g protein | 4.4g carbs | 1.7g fiber | 0.4g sugar | 2mg sodium

. . . .

PREP: 5 minutes
YIELDS: 10 tablespoons

. . . .

3 tablespoons (24g) paprika
2 tablespoons (22g) garlic powder
1½ tablespoons (16g) onion powder
1½ tablespoons (5g) dried thyme
1½ tablespoons (4g) dried oregano
2 teaspoons (6g) ground black pepper
2 teaspoons (6g) cayenne pepper

CURRY SPICE BLEND

PREP: 5 minutes
YIELDS: ½ cup

. . . .

3 tablespoons (25g) turmeric

3 tablespoons (16g) ground
    coriander

1 tablespoon + ½ teaspoon (8g)
    ground cumin

1½ teaspoons (5g) garlic powder

¾ teaspoon (2g) ground
    cinnamon

¾ teaspoon (2g) cayenne
    pepper

¾ teaspoon (2g) ground ginger

¼ + ⅛ teaspoon (1g) ground
    nutmeg

1½ teaspoons (4g) ground black
    pepper

OPTIONAL: good pinch of
    ground cloves

Keep this curry blend on hand for quick curries and soups. I use it for any recipe calling for standard yellow curry powder, and it tastes better than store-bought. I love curry powder in my Protein-Packed Curry Chickpeas and Sweet Potato Rounds on page 118.

Add all of the spices to a small bowl, and whisk very well. Store the blend in a sealed jar for up to 6 months.

. . . .

Nutrition per tablespoon: 18 calories | 0.6g fat | 0.6g protein | 3.2g carbs | 1g fiber | 0.3g sugar | 3mg sodium

. . . .

oil free • gluten free • nut free

DIY HOMEMADE CHILI POWDER

It can be very hard to find a standard American-style chili powder in many countries other than the United States, so for all of you who have trouble finding it, I have created a DIY blend. Standard American chili powder is a blend of different spices while chili powders in other countries are strictly all peppers and are very hot. Use this blend in any recipe calling for mild chili powder.

Add all of the ingredients to a small bowl, and whisk very well. Alternatively, add them to a jar with a tight-fitting lid and shake vigorously to ensure even mixing. Store in a cool, dry place for up to 6 months.

. . . .

Nutrition per tablespoon: 21 calories | 0.8g fat | 1g protein | 4g carbs | 2.2g fiber | 0.8g sugar | 17mg sodium

. . . .

PREP: 5 minutes
YIELDS: about 6 tablespoons

. . . .

3½ tablespoons (28g) paprika
3½ teaspoons (14g) ancho chile powder
1 teaspoon (1g) dried oregano
1 teaspoon (4g) garlic powder
1 teaspoon (4g) onion powder
½ teaspoon (1g) ground cumin

CASHEWS 3 WAYS

PREP: 3 minutes
YIELDS: 3⅔ cups

. . . .

1 cup (140g) raw, unsalted cashews
3 cups (720g) filtered water

❧ *tip* ☙

If you do not have a high-powered blender like a Vitamix, you'll need to soak your cashews for 8 hours or preferably overnight in a bowl of warm water to soften, and then drain, rinse, and proceed with the recipe. Otherwise, the finished product will be gritty. If using soaked cashews, a food processor works better than a regular, non-high-powered blender.

HOMEMADE CASHEW MILK

Store-bought cashew milk is just so sad. It is watered down, full of yucky additives, and doesn't even *begin* to compare to homemade. Try making a sauce with this homemade cashew milk and then with a store-bought version. The differences will be glaringly obvious. Not only will my version thicken incredibly better, but the taste is richer, creamier, and fresher. I love to use the cashew milk for thickening soups, as with my Cajun Veggie and Potato Chowder on page 158. It imparts the most amazing texture. This takes barely 5 minutes to make if you have a high-powered blender. If you do not, you will need to soak your cashews in a bowl of water overnight for the best results. We don't want gritty milk, now do we?

Add the cashews and 3 cups (720g) filtered water to a high-powered blender or food processor (if using soaked cashews, see Tip at right), and blend on high until completely smooth. Pour into a container with a tight-fitting lid and store in the fridge for up to 3 days. It is normal for settling to occur, so just give it a good stir before each use. If you are using a blender that is not very powerful, you will need to blend the mixture for as long as you can to get it smooth, then strain it well through a fine strainer.

. . . .

Nutrition per ½ cup: 134 calories | 10.8g fat | 3.6g protein | 7.6g carbs | 0.7g fiber | 1.2g sugar | 4mg sodium

. . . .

PREP: 3 minutes
YIELDS: 1⅔ cups

. . . .

1 cup (140g) raw, unsalted cashews
1 cup (240g) filtered water

HOMEMADE CASHEW CREAM

To make the cashew cream, the same steps above apply, only the amounts differ. You may need to scrape the sides a couple of times to get the mixture totally smooth. If you do not have a high-powered blender, a food processor will work better for the cashew cream. The cream can be used in coffee or sauces where a really thick result is desired.

. . . .

Nutrition per tablespoon: 50 calories | 4.1g fat | 1.3g protein | 2.9g carbs | 0.3g fiber | 0.4g sugar | 1mg sodium

. . . .

oil free • gluten free

HOMEMADE CASHEW BUTTER

To make cashew butter, no soaking or water is needed. I store cashew butter in the pantry as it keeps the texture soft, making it ready for immediate use. Stored in the fridge it will last longer, of course, but it gets very hard. Let it come to room temperature before using in a recipe. My favorite way to use it is in my 20-Minute Alfredo on page 68 and Silky Smooth Chive and Dill Cream Cheese on page 47.

Add the cashews to a food processor (not a blender), and process for 5 to 10 minutes. The cashew butter will go through stages, and you will need to stop and push the cashews down the sides and break up clumps a few times in the beginning. Keep processing until it has a thick, creamy consistency, and then process even further until it is no longer stiff. You will want to keep going until the cashew butter is soft and flowy, almost like a frosting. It should drip off of a spoon. Store the cashew butter in an airtight container in the pantry for up to 2 weeks or in the fridge for up to 2 months.

Nutrition per tablespoon: 100 calories | 8.1g fat | 2.7g protein | 5.7g carbs | 0.5g fiber | 0.9g sugar | 3mg sodium

PREP: 5 minutes
YIELDS: heaping 1 cup

2 cups (280g) raw, unsalted cashews

❧ METRIC EQUIVALENTS ❧

COOKING/OVEN TEMPERATURES

	FAHRENHEIT	CELSIUS	GAS MARK
Freeze Water	32° F	0° C	
Room Temp.	68° F	20° C	
Boil Water	212° F	100° C	
Bake	325° F	160° C	3
	350° F	180° C	4
	375° F	190° C	5
	400° F	200° C	6
	425° F	220° C	7
	450° F	230° C	8
Broil			Grill

LIQUID INGREDIENTS BY VOLUME

¼ tsp	=						1 ml		
½ tsp	=						2 ml		
1 tsp	=						5 ml		
3 tsp	=	1 Tbsp	=	½ fl oz	=		15 ml		
2 Tbsp	=	⅛ cup	=	1 fl oz	=		30 ml		
4 Tbsp	=	¼ cup	=	2 fl oz	=		60 ml		
5⅓ Tbsp	=	⅓ cup	=	3 fl oz	=		80 ml		
8 Tbsp	=	½ cup	=	4 fl oz	=		120 ml		
10⅔ Tbsp	=	⅔ cup	=	5 fl oz	=		160 ml		
12 Tbsp	=	¾ cup	=	6 fl oz	=		180 ml		
16 Tbsp	=	1 cup	=	8 fl oz	=		240 ml		
1 pt	=	2 cups	=	16 fl oz	=		480 ml		
1 qt	=	4 cups	=	32 fl oz	=		960 ml		
				33 fl oz	=	1000 ml		=	1 l

DRY INGREDIENTS BY WEIGHT

(To convert ounces to grams,
multiply the number of ounces by 30.)

1 oz	=	¹⁄₁₆ lb	=	30 g
4 oz	=	¼ lb	=	120 g
8 oz	=	½ lb	=	240 g
12 oz	=	¾ lb	=	360 g
16 oz	=	1 lb	=	480 g

LENGTH

(To convert inches to centimeters,
multiply inches by 2.5.)

1 in	=					2.5 cm		
12 in	=	1 ft			=	30 cm		
36 in	=	3 ft	=	1 yd	=	90 cm		
40 in	=					100 cm	=	1m

EQUIVALENTS FOR DIFFERENT TYPES OF INGREDIENTS

STANDARD CUP	FINE POWDER (EX. FLOUR)	GRAIN (EX. RICE)	GRANULAR (EX. SUGAR)	LIQUID SOLIDS (EX. BUTTER)	LIQUID (EX. MILK)
1	140 g	150 g	190 g	200 g	240 ml
¾	105 g	113 g	143 g	150 g	180 ml
⅔	93 g	100 g	125 g	133 g	160 ml
½	70 g	75 g	95 g	100 g	120 ml
⅓	47 g	50 g	63 g	67 g	80 ml
¼	35 g	38 g	48 g	50 g	60 ml
⅛	18 g	19 g	24 g	25 g	30 ml

INDEX

ACKNOWLEDGMENTS

There were so many amazing people who helped to make this book happen. I want to give you all a big hug!

Thank you to my wonderful husband, Jay, and my daughter, Olivia. Without you, Jay, and that darn gout, this book never would have happened. My desire to heal you is what brought us here. Thank you for your endless encouragement, jokes, and constant reminder of "you can do this" when I consistently got stressed-out and was expressing self-doubt. You continued to give me ideas and tell me I could do it. I love you. To my angel Olivia, honey, I love you so much. I can't even put into words how much I love you. Your patience with my extra workload these past several months made me so proud. You recognized that I was doing something important to me and were so patient. I'm so happy to have more free time again. Thank you both for your endless love and the constant taste testing of food that I was shoving into your faces daily.

Thank you Mom and Dad for testing several recipes, always providing honest feedback, and, most importantly, believing in me. Thank you for being there and showing understanding toward the end when I was so swamped I couldn't even spare a moment. Thank you for your love, patience, and belief in my abilities. I love you.

Kacy Allensworth, my best friend, a huge thank you for cheering me on from that first phone call I made to you about my new website idea for The Vegan 8 and its crazy concept. You believed in me from the get-go and have always been so supportive. I love you!

Estee Hammer, you are an amazing friend and the ultimate taste tester. What would I do without you? I seriously could not have completed this book without you and your boys. You tested nearly every single recipe in this book without one complaint and always provided valuable feedback. I am so grateful to you and your boys. You listened to me, encouraged me, and never let me give up. You motivated me every time I had self-doubt. Thank you for being a friend and therapist, ha ha.

Thank you to all of my taste testers for your amazing and valuable feedback to help make this book so amazing. All of you, your kids, and your husbands all provided wonderful and detailed opinions and tips that helped me out so much during the testing process. I value each and every one of you and cannot express my gratitude enough! Thank you to Stacy Novosat, Ellen Lederman, Sharon Vega, Mary Jean Kersey, Dawn Samson, Moalyne Honore, Jessica Maria Britt, Marie Brown, Bridget Young, Anni Turnbull, and Linda Atkinson.

Thank you to Rachel West, my editor, you've been so caring and so patient and listened to every detail of how I wanted this book to look and turn out. I'm so grateful to you and the whole team at Oxmoor House!

Last but certainly not least, thank you, Elvis Presley. Thank you to your beautiful voice and music blaring throughout my kitchen over months of testing so many recipes. Your music kept my spirits up and made the constant workload a bit more bearable. Your music has helped me through times as a child all the way through writing my first cookbook!